500

breakfasts & brunches

500

breakfasts & brunches

Carol Beckerman

A Quintet Book

First published in the UK in 2011 by
Apple Press
7 Greenland Street
London NW1 0ND
United Kingdom

www.apple-press.com

ISBN: 978-1-84543-381-9
QTT.FHBB

This book was conceived, designed, and produced by
Quintet Publishing Limited
6 Blundell Street
London N7 9BH
United Kingdom

Food Stylists: Carol Beckerman, Valentina Sforza
Photographer: Ian Garlick
Art Director: Michael Charles
Editorial Assistants: Carly Beckerman-Boys, Holly Willsher
Managing Editor: Donna Gregory
Publisher: James Tavendale

10 9 8 7 6 5 4 3 2 1

Printed in China by 1010 Printing International Ltd.

contents

introduction

Eat breakfast...be happy! People often say they skip breakfast because they do not have time, or simply because they are not hungry. But cliché or not, breakfast is certainly the most important meal of the day. When you wake up in the morning, you will not have eaten for about twelve hours, so your body is like a car that has run out of petrol. You need fuel, and you need it first thing in the morning if you want to get the most out of your day.

Without a doubt, breakfast provides the energy we need for daily life, boosting the metabolism and getting the body burning calories efficiently. It provides essential vitamins and nutrients, and it can also help you maintain your weight. There is some evidence to suggest that children and adults who eat breakfast regularly perform better and are less likely to be overweight than those who do not. Also, skipping breakfast is strongly linked to the development of obesity. Studies show that overweight and obese children, adolescents and adults are less likely to eat breakfast than their slimmer counterparts.

The average working woman and man needs around 2,100 and 2,800 calories a day respectively, and if you are engaged in heavy physical work or exercise, you will need more. If you spread out your calorie intake sensibly over three meals per day, you should be thinking of eating a breakfast comprising around 800 or 1,000 calories.

While adults need breakfast, children need it even more. When they skip breakfast, they can end up going for as long as 18 hours without food, taking into account that an evening

meal will probably be eaten around 6 p.m., and lunch the next day will not arrive until roughly noon. This period of semistarvation can create a lot of physical, intellectual and behavioural problems. If you or your children regularly skip breakfast, remember that eating a wholesome, nutritious morning meal will probably save you time in the long run.

By recharging your brain and your body, you will be more efficient in just about everything that you do. Not eating breakfast tends to make you tired and lethargic, encourages you to eat more at your next meal and can cause you to snack on high-calorie, less nutritious foods to stave off hunger.

One reason people give for skipping breakfast is that they do not know what to eat. This book will show you how diverse the possibilities are when considering your breakfast menu.

Whether you have breakfast in a leisurely fashion at home, on the run or at work, you will find lots of ideas to build on. From romantic breakfasts in bed to brown-bagged breakfast sandwiches and brunches with family and friends, all the recipes are found here, in one easy-to-use book.

breakfasts from around the world

Adding to the diverse collection of dishes found in this book, there are many new flavour combinations and exciting recipes from around the world. Breakfasts tend to be very different depending on country and culture of origin.

In Poland, for example, a substantial platter for breakfast is usually served. This includes cold meats, meat pastes, polish sausage, sardines, tomatoes and sliced pickles, eaten with an array of side dishes. In some countries, China for instance, the same food is eaten for breakfast, lunch and dinner. Generally speaking, it is rice eaten with small amounts of vegetables and meat. In Japan, many people eat a Western-style breakfast – but traditionally breakfast would consist of steamed rice, miso soup and various side dishes. Boiled or grilled fish, omelettes and dried seaweed might also be served.

In Malaysia, a popular breakfast is called *nasi lemek*, which is simply rice, cooked in coconut milk, with various extra ingredients tossed into the pot to add fragrance. It is available on just about every street corner and in almost every local restaurant, served with chicken or beef and even cuttlefish. Malaysians also like *kaya*, a sort of jelly made with eggs, sugar and coconut milk, which is spread on toast.

In Europe, you will find the countries that define the term 'continental breakfast'. These countries eat a large lunch, and the first meal of the day is the absolute minimum of stimulant and sustenance: coffee and bread. In France, the popular choice is café au lait, served in large ceramic bowls. The bread is usually a croissant, brioche or a slice of toast, with butter and good-quality fruit jam. Another popular choice is hot chocolate.

Germans like something a bit more substantial – a selection of freshly baked rolls, which will often be served with a generous selection of cold meats, cheeses, fruit and yoghurt. Bavarian sausages are popular, made from finely minced veal and fresh bacon.

Breakfast in Italy is generally sweet. Cake is a traditional Italian breakfast food, as are cookies. There is no tradition in Italy of savoury food on the breakfast table, and hot coffee or cappuccino is served with pastries, brioche, croissants or toast.

The Spanish like to have a light breakfast and a large lunch too. Here breakfast is the smallest meal of the day. They like sweet rolls called magdalenas, lemon cupcakes and sugary, deep-fried churros with chocolate.

In Finland they eat a pancake called *panmi kakku*, which is made from batter using evaporated milk. In Slovakia, it would be salami and cheese, eaten with bread rolls and butter. Some people have mustard with it, some prefer onion.

The Romanian cuisine is very diverse. It includes a lot of customs and culinary traditions, having been influenced along the way by other nationalities it has come into contact with. These would include the Turks, Hungarians and Slavs. There is no traditional first meal of the day in Romania, so it varies from region to region. In the cities, people grab whatever is quick, whereas in the countryside, they eat something called *mamaliga*, a sort of semolina mush, served with cold milk. They also eat bread, dairy products, vegetables, tomatoes, onions and eggs. A continental breakfast is much more popular in Romania now than it used to be.

The British love their traditional fry-up, served more often these days at the weekend, when everyone has more time. The bacon is back bacon, more meaty and less fatty than American bacon. The sausages are thick and meaty, and the eggs good quality and as large as possible.

Australians eat a similar breakfast to the British, with the unexpected addition of kangaroo sausages. You will also find popovers, and Australians love toast thickly covered with a strong-tasting, salty spread made from yeast extract.

In New Zealand, most restaurants will have at least one menu option served with grilled bananas, a delicious accompaniment to French toast, which is good made with slightly aged Arizmendi bread.

equipment

You do not need a lot of special equipment for making breakfast. At least one good-quality large frying pan, preferably nonstick and oven-safe, is a must. You probably already have pots, baking trays and baking pans (32x22cm/9x13in) is about the right size for many of these recipes, although a couple use a slightly smaller one).

For smoothies, you will need a blender (one that crushes ice would be helpful). Pancakes can be made in a large frying pan, or on a griddle and waffles have to be made in a waffle iron. For muffins you need a 12-cup muffin pan, and use paper muffin liners – these keep the muffins together nicely.

When making yeast bread, it is very easy to learn the technique of kneading; however, a freestanding tabletop mixer gets the job done quickly and efficiently. It will turn out perfect bread every time.

You will need a whisk for whisking eggs, although for lightly beaten eggs you can use a dinner fork. A pastry brush to apply oil, butter and various toppings will be needed as well.

ingredients

The ingredients needed to make the recipes in this book are pretty standard fare for most kitchens. I do, however, call for buttermilk in my baked goods, which might be new to you.

buttermilk

Buttermilk is a wonderful dairy product that makes delicious baked goods. It was first called buttermilk because it was originally the liquid left over after the butter-churning process was finished. Despite its name, it is low in fat.

It is a rich-tasting, thick and tangy milk, with a buttery flavour. Like yoghurt and sour cream, it helps tenderise the gluten in a batter, giving a softer texture and more body, and helping baked goods to rise. It gives a pleasant tang and buttery flavour to pancakes and baked goods, without adding lots of butter or fat. Buttermilk is acidic, so bicarbonate of soda is added to the recipe to balance the acid.

Buttermilk is sold in smaller containers than milk, and it has a longer shelf life, so you have more time to use it. It tends to thicken with time, so shake the carton before use.

eggs

Use the freshest eggs for poaching and frying and leave the less fresh for baking. Buy organic eggs if you can; they have higher levels of vitamins E and A, and they taste better and have a richer colour.

There are three ways to test whether an egg is fresh. First, hold the egg in your hand and shake gently. If you feel a rattle, it is not very fresh. In a newly laid egg, the air cell within the egg is very small, the white cushions the yolk, and the egg feels solid and quite heavy when shaken.

The second way is to gently drop the egg, without breaking, into a deep bowl of water. If the egg immediately sinks to the bottom and lies on its side, the egg is fresh. As an egg ages, more air permeates the shell, and it will begin to float and stand upright. If it floats without touching the bottom of the bowl at all, do not eat it as it is probably bad.

The third way to test for freshness is to break the egg onto a flat plate. A fresh yolk will sit high on the white in the middle and the white will be thick and stay close to the yolk. As an egg gets older, the white becomes more runny and will spread over the plate, and the yolk will break more easily. If the white is cloudy, it means the egg is very fresh. Store eggs in the refrigerator for up to one month, in the carton, which helps prevent them from absorbing food odours.

meats
All the meats used in this book can be found in ordinary supermarkets. Use the best-quality bacon and sausages you can find. I've included a recipe for making your own sausage, which allows you to control the amount of fat, salt and preservatives that you eat.

oils, butter & margarine

You can use most oils, butter or margarine for most of these recipes. My personal preference is vegetable oil. If you have heart problems, you need to keep your consumption of hard fats like butter and margarine to a minimum. Much better for you is a fat that is runny when cold, and vegetable oil is the best of the lot. It's even better than olive oil, which although better for you than butter, is quite strong-tasting. It has too powerful a flavour for cooking pancakes and waffles. You can also use sunflower oil, a delicate oil ideal for cooking pancakes or using in muffins. If you are trying to keep to a low-fat diet, it is quite acceptable to use a spray oil in your frying pan.

flour & sugar

All recipes in this book use plain flour, unless otherwise specified. Use the type of sugar called for in the recipes. When it is not specified, granulated sugar is intended.

nuts, seeds & dried fruits

Nuts and seeds add amazing variety and crunch to bread, cereals, muffins and even pancakes and waffles. Walnuts especially are good for your heart, but not too many as they are high in calories (four walnuts a day is ideal). The nuts and seeds used in these recipes are unroasted and unsalted and should be easy to find. Keep them in an airtight container, in a cool place, for optimum freshness. Dried fruits also need to be kept in airtight containers in a cool place.

techniques

muffins

The secret to good muffins is a very simple one. Mix all the wet ingredients in one bowl, and all the dry ingredients in another bowl. Treat fresh fruit as a dry ingredient, canned fruit as wet (except for canned or very ripe blueberries, which have to be added at the last possible moment because they crush very easily).

When you have your ingredients ready in their bowls, make a well in the centre of the dry ingredients with a metal spoon or a fork, and pour the wet ingredients into the middle. Fold the two together as quickly and lightly as you can, until they are just blended. Do not worry about small dry lumps that may remain. Spoon batter into paper-lined muffin pans immediately, filling the cups about ¾ full. Put the pan directly into the oven. The end result will be light and airy muffins.

pancakes

The same idea works for pancakes too. Mix dry ingredients in one bowl, wet in another, and then mix together as with muffins. The small lumps do not matter; it is more important to work the batter as little as possible. After making one or two pancakes, you will begin to get an idea of what to watch for when cooking them.

When you have spooned a measure of batter into the frying pan and it sizzles and begins to cook, it will start to form small bubbles and look dry around the edge of the pancake. It will start to rise very slightly in the middle, and that is the time to turn it over. It will start to look light and risen as it cooks. When the pancake is done, it should be a lovely golden brown colour and feel considerably lighter as you lift it.

crepes

Unlike pancakes, the thinner crêpe has a different look and feel. It is quicker to cook and easier to burn. It takes a little more practice to perfect the technique for a crêpe, but after making one or two, you will get the idea very quickly.

The batter needs to be spooned into the lightly oiled frying pan, and then swirled around the pan so that it just covers the surface. The pan should be very hot, but not smoking, before you pour in the batter, then you need to get it back on the heat immediately. Watch carefully, because it will cook quickly, but it should not stick to the pan. It should be easy to flip over to cook the other side.

bread

All around the world, bread is the popular choice for breakfast. Once you have mastered the art of bread making, you will be hooked. As mentioned earlier, a freestanding tabletop mixer is a handy appliance to have in your kitchen, but kneading dough by hand is a very satisfying occupation. You start making yeast bread with a yeast liquid. Add a teaspoon of sugar to warm water or milk, and add dry yeast. Leave the liquid to stand for about 15 minutes, until it is very frothy. The better the froth, the better the rise of the dough. (The dough should never rise more than double in size, however.)

When you are mixing your dough, watch the consistency of the flour and water. If the dough is too sticky (it sticks to your fingers), add a little more flour. If the dough seems too dry, add a tiny bit more water. Place the dough on a floured surface, and lightly flour your hands. Push the heel of your hands into the middle of the dough with a sharp movement, almost like a punch. Slightly roll the dough as you do so. With each push, turn the dough a half turn and knead again. Continue working the dough with your fingers and knuckles, until it becomes smooth and elastic. This is a technique that is quickly acquired once you start the process.

When the dough feels smooth, place it in a large, greased bowl, and turn the dough over so that it is completely covered with a thin film of oil. This is to stop it from forming a hard crust. Cover the bowl with cling film and set it aside to rise until the dough has doubled in size. If you have time to let it rise, leave it at room temperature. If you have a lot of time, leave it overnight in the refrigerator; if you are short on time, leave it in a warm place. When it has doubled in size, put the dough onto a lightly floured surface, punch down to remove air bubbles, and then follow the specific recipe.

drinks, smoothies & yoghurt

Fruit juices and smoothies are a great way of getting children to eat fruit and vegetables. For the grownups, sophisticated coffee and smooth, rich, decadent hot chocolate are delicious alternatives. Try a bellini or Bloody Mary for celebrations and weekend treats.

wake-up juice

see variations page 45

Start the day off right by firing up the circulation and kicking off the body's cleansing process.

2 large oranges   125g (4oz) fresh strawberries
1 pink grapefruit   ½ banana

Squeeze the juice from the oranges and grapefruit. Pour juice into a blender, add the strawberries and banana and blend well. Pour the juice into glasses and serve.

Serves 2

bloody mary

see variations page 46

The Bloody Mary is great as a starter for any breakfast or brunch. It is also great as a hangover cure!

50ml (2fl.oz) vodka
150ml (5fl.oz) tomato juice
1 tbsp lemon juice
2 dashes Worcestershire sauce

2 drops hot pepper sauce, such as Tabasco
pinch salt
pinch freshly ground black pepper
celery stalk, to garnish

Place all the ingredients, except the celery, into a cocktail shaker with 3 cubes of ice and shake well. Strain into a highball glass, being careful not to allow any ice to fall into the glass as this would dilute the cocktail. Garnish with the celery stick, which you eat between sips to enhance the flavour.

Serves 1

celebration breakfast bellini

see variations page 47

Traditionally this cocktail is made with puréed white peaches and Italian sparkling wine, with a little raspberry or cherry juice to give it a pink glow. Ideally you want one-third peach purée to two-thirds champagne.

2 ripe peaches, peeled, halved and pitted
2 tsp raspberry juice (optional)
chilled champagne

Chill 2 champagne glasses in your refrigerator. Put the peaches in a blender and purée until completely smooth. Spoon about 50g (2oz) of the purée into a chilled champagne glass, add the raspberry juice if using, and top off with champagne. Serve immediately.

Serves 2

easy home-brewed cappuccino

see variations page 48

A cafetière works well for this recipe. You'll also need a handheld stick whisk.

coffee beans (see method)
225ml (8fl.oz) milk
1 tsp sugar, or to taste
1 tsp grated plain (or a favourite) chocolate, for
    sprinkling

Make enough coffee for 2 mugs. Grind the beans just before you need them and use extra beans so your coffee is extra-strong.

Microwave the milk and sugar in a glass microwave-safe cup until almost boiling. Alternatively, heat it in a small saucepan on top of the stove. Pour 175ml (6fl.oz) of the hot, sweetened milk into your mug with the coffee. Use your handheld whisk to whip the remaining milk in the glass cup until frothy, then pour it on top of the coffee. Sprinkle with grated chocolate.

Serves 2

spiced hot coffee

see variations page 49

Plain coffee is delicious, but sometimes you just want something different – especially on a cold winter day when you need some extra heat.

225ml (8fl.oz) water
1 cinnamon stick
6 cardamom pods, split
6 black peppercorns
125ml (4fl.oz) double cream

3 tbsp brown sugar
450ml (16fl.oz) freshly brewed coffee
freshly grated nutmeg, to serve

In a small saucepan, combine the water and the spices. Bring to the boil, then reduce the heat and simmer for 5 minutes. Add the cream and sugar and stir. Add the coffee, increase the heat, and bring to just under boiling. Remove from the heat and strain into mugs. Serve immediately, sprinkled with nutmeg.

Serves 1-2

rich & creamy hot chocolate

see variations page 50

The better the quality of chocolate used, the better the taste. Always use whole milk to get a fuller, more rounded, creamy flavour.

1.5 litres (2½ pints) whole milk
50ml (2fl.oz) whipping cream
25g (1oz) unsweetened cocoa powder
50g (2oz) sugar
pinch salt

125g (4oz) bitter or plain chocolate, chopped
whipped cream and miniature marshmallows,
    to serve

In a medium saucepan, bring the milk and whipping cream to just simmering with the cocoa, sugar and salt. Add the chopped chocolate, whisking all the time until the mixture becomes frothy. Ladle into 4 mugs, and top with whipped cream and marshmallows.

Serves 4

mocha shake

see variations page 51

If you can never decide between coffee and chocolate, this will solve your problem. It's rich, thick and absolutely divine.

1.5 litres (2½ pints) milk
90g (3½oz) plain chocolate, broken

1 tbsp instant coffee granules
4 scoops vanilla ice cream

Bring 350ml (12fl.oz) of milk almost to the boil in a saucepan, then add the chocolate and the coffee granules and stir until melted. Set aside to cool.

Just before serving, pour the mixture into a blender with the ice cream and the remaining milk, and blend until smooth.

Serves 3-4

multi-berry smoothie

see variations page 52

Mixed berry smoothies contain a high level of antioxidants and vitamins, so not only do they taste wonderful but they are also good for you. If you use frozen berries, you'll have a frozen smoothie, a great way to treat yourself on a hot summer day.

125g (4oz) fresh or frozen blueberries
125g (4oz) fresh or frozen strawberries
125g (4oz) fresh or frozen raspberries
175ml (6fl.oz) milk (whole or semi-skimmed)
2 tbsp low-fat natural yoghurt

2 tbsp freshly squeezed orange juice
1 tbsp honey
1 tbsp wheatgerm
a little sugar to taste (optional)

Put the blueberries into a blender and purée until smooth. Add the strawberries and raspberries and blend again. Add the rest of the ingredients, blend, then pour into glasses and serve.

Serves 2

protein smoothie

see variations page 53

The protein powder in this smoothie helps you start your day feeling energised.

1 banana
½ mango, peeled, seeded and chopped
125g (4oz) chopped fresh or tinned pineapple
1 serving protein powder

125ml (4fl.oz) orange juice (preferably freshly
    squeezed)
4 ice cubes

Put the fruits together in a blender and blend briefly. Add the protein powder (checking directions on the package) and blend again. Add the orange juice, blend, then add the ice cubes and blend again until smooth. Pour into a large glass and serve.

Serves 1

greek yoghurt

see variations page 54

This might, at first glance, look complicated, but the effort is well worth it. Remember to keep a small amount of yoghurt aside to make the next batch.

900ml (1½ pints) plus 3 tbsp whole milk, either
goat's or cow's
3 tbsp live yoghurt

Have all the ingredients at room temperature. Heat 900ml (1½ pints) milk just to boiling point, then pour into a non-metallic container. Let it cool to lukewarm, about 43°C (110°F). A skin will form on top as the milk cools.

Mix the yoghurt with the remaining 3 tablespoons room-temperature milk, then add the mixture to the lukewarm milk, carefully pouring it into the bowl down the sides so that you do not disturb the skin on top. Cover bowl with a clean tea towel and place it on another tea towel in a warm, dry place for at least 8 hours, or overnight, until it thickens (8–12 hours is best). The longer you leave the yoghurt after 12 hours, the more sour it will become.

Carefully drain off any excess liquid. Refrigerate for at least 4 hours before serving. It will keep for 4-5 days. Remember to save a small amount to make the next batch!

You can eat the yoghurt, as well as the skin on top, now. Alternatively, you can proceed to the next step to make the thick yoghurt used in so many Greek recipes. Line a large bowl with a piece of cheesecloth or a clean white tea towel. Pour the yoghurt into the centre of the cloth. Bring the four corners of the cloth together and lift the yoghurt. Over the sink,

twist the corners to squeeze out the liquid through the cloth. When you have forced out the majority of the liquid, tie off the top of the cloth, above the mass of yoghurt, with string.

Place in a colander or sieve over a bowl so the liquid can continue to drain, and place the whole thing in the refrigerator for 2-3 hours. After draining, put the cloth with the yoghurt inside the sink and with your hands, force out any remaining liquid. Remove the string, open the cloth, and, using a spatula, put the yoghurt in a bowl for use. The yoghurt should have the consistency of soured cream.
Makes about 450g (1lb)

apricot–oat smoothie

see variations page 55

Smoothies made with oats satisfy hunger and help lower cholesterol. Strong-tasting spices also help to make you feel full.

350g (12oz) tinned apricots, drained
3 tbsp instant porridge oats
350ml (12fl.oz) cold milk

1 tsp ground ginger
1 tsp ground cinnamon
1 tbsp honey

Put the apricots into a blender and purée. Add all the other ingredients and blend until smooth. Pour into glasses and serve.

Serves 2

wake-up juice

see base recipe page 27

orange & lemon wake-up juice
Prepare the basic recipe, omitting the grapefruit and adding the juice of
2 more oranges and 1 lemon.

orange, lemon & pineapple wake-up juice
Prepare the basic recipe, omitting the grapefruit and adding the juice of
½ lemon. Add 225g (8oz) chopped tinned or fresh pineapple and blend until
smooth.

orange & cranberry wake-up juice
Prepare the basic recipe, omitting the grapefruit and substituting 450g (1lb) fresh
or frozen cranberries. Add a little sugar, if desired, to taste.

mixed berry wake-up juice
Prepare the basic recipe, omitting the grapefruit and adding 225g (8oz) fresh or
frozen mixed berries.

tropical wake-up juice
Prepare the basic recipe, omitting the grapefruit. Substitute ½ mango, peeled,
pitted and chopped; 225g (8oz) chopped pineapple; and another ½ banana.

variations

bloody mary

see base recipe page 28

bloody maria
Prepare the basic recipe, replacing the vodka with 50ml (2fl.oz) tequila.

bloody mary with coriander
Prepare the basic recipe, adding 1 teaspoon finely chopped fresh coriander.

mustard mary
Prepare the basic recipe, adding ½ teaspoon French mustard.

virgin mary
Prepare the basic recipe, omitting the vodka.

soy sauce mary
Prepare the basic recipe, replacing the Worcestershire sauce with dark soy sauce.

celebration breakfast bellini

see base recipe page 31

italian bellini
Prepare the basic recipe, replacing the champagne with Italian sparkling wine.

bellini martini
Instead of the basic recipe, pour 50ml (2fl.oz) vodka and 50ml (2fl.oz) peach schnapps into a cocktail shaker with 225g (8oz) ice. Shake until frothy, then strain into a martini glass. Top the glass off with about 50ml (2fl.oz) champagne. Garnish with 3 fresh raspberries.

virgin bellini
Prepare the basic recipe, replacing the champagne with sparkling apple juice.

frozen bellini
Instead of the basic recipe, blend 1 part peach schnapps with 3 parts champagne and freeze until slushy, about 2 hours. In a large glass, put a tinned or peeled fresh peach half, add 120ml (4fl.oz) slush, and carefully pour a little sangria on top to add a dash of colour.

variations

easy home-brewed cappuccino

see base recipe page 32

vanilla cappuccino
Prepare the basic recipe, adding 1 teaspoon vanilla extract to each mug along with the milk and coffee.

iced cappuccino
Prepare the basic recipe, replacing 50ml (2fl.oz) of the milk with 50ml (2fl.oz) double cream and making the coffee double strength. Allow the cappuccino to cool to room temperature, then put all the ingredients in a blender with 4 ice cubes and blend until smooth.

cinnamon-spiced cappuccino
Prepare the basic recipe, adding 1 teaspoon ground cinnamon to the mug with the milk and coffee. Replace the chocolate with a sprinkling of ground cinnamon.

chocolate–orange cappuccino
Prepare the basic recipe, replacing the grated chocolate with plenty of grated orange-flavoured chocolate.

ginger-spiced cappuccino
Prepare the basic recipe, adding 1 teaspoon ground ginger to the mug with the milk and coffee.

variations

spiced hot coffee

see base recipe page 34

nutmeg-spiced coffee
Prepare the basic recipe, replacing the cardamom pods and black peppercorns with ¼ teaspoon ground cloves and ¼ teaspoon ground nutmeg.

vanilla-spiced coffee
Prepare the basic recipe, omitting the cardamom pods and black peppercorns and adding ½ teaspoon vanilla extract.

fall-spiced coffee
Prepare the basic recipe, replacing the cardamom pods and black peppercorns with ¼ teaspoon pumpkin pie or mixed spice.

honey-spiced coffee
Prepare the basic recipe, omitting the cardamom pods and black peppercorns and adding 2 teaspoons honey.

cocoa-spiced coffee
Prepare the basic recipe, omitting the cardamom pods and black peppercorns and adding ½ teaspoon vanilla extract and 1 teaspoon unsweetened cocoa powder.

variations

rich & creamy hot chocolate

see base recipe page 35

rich & creamy hot chocolate with cinnamon
Prepare the basic recipe, and add a cinnamon stick to each mug as
you serve.

rich & creamy hot chocolate with vanilla
Prepare the basic recipe, and add 1 teaspoon vanilla extract to the saucepan
just before serving.

rich & creamy hot chocolate with grand marnier
Prepare the basic recipe, and add 2 tablespoons Grand Marnier to the
saucepan just before serving.

rich, creamy & spicy hot chocolate
Prepare the basic recipe, and add ½ teaspoon chilli powder to the saucepan
just before serving.

fudgy, rich & creamy hot chocolate
Prepare the basic recipe, replacing half the sugar with brown sugar. (It may
not sound very different, but the brown sugar makes the hot chocolate taste
like chocolate fudge.)

mocha shake

see base recipe page 37

double chocolate shake
Prepare the basic recipe, replacing the coffee granules and the vanilla ice cream with 4 scoops of chocolate ice cream.

chocolate cherry shake
Prepare the basic recipe, replacing the coffee granules and the vanilla ice cream with 4 scoops of cherry or other berry ice cream and 50g (2oz) fresh or tinned pitted cherries.

non-dairy chocolate coconut shake
Prepare the basic recipe, replacing the milk with 700ml (1¼ pints) coconut milk. Check that the plain chocolate that you use contains no dairy products.

mocha banana shake
Prepare the basic recipe, adding 1 banana to the ingredients.

rich mocha shake
Prepare the basic recipe, using only 600ml (1 pint) milk and adding 125ml (4fl.oz) double cream.

variations

multi-berry smoothie

see base recipe page 38

apple blackberry smoothie
Prepare the basic recipe, omitting the blueberries. Add ½ peeled and chopped apple and 125g (4oz) blackberries. Add a little extra sugar to taste, if desired.

nondairy berry smoothie
Prepare the basic recipe, replacing the milk and the yoghurt with coconut milk and soya yoghurt.

quick berry banana smoothie
Prepare the basic recipe, omitting the milk, honey and wheatgerm. Increase the amount of yoghurt and orange juice to 225ml (8fl.oz) of each, and add ½ banana.

tropical smoothie
Prepare the basic recipe, omitting the orange juice and blueberries and adding 125g (4oz) chopped fresh or tinned pineapple and ½ mango, peeled, pitted and chopped.

protein smoothie

see base recipe page 41

dairy peach melba protein smoothie
Prepare the basic recipe, omitting the orange juice, pineapple and mango.
Substitute 225g (8oz) sliced and peeled fresh or tinned peaches, 50g (2oz) fresh
raspberries, and 125ml (4fl.oz) whole milk.

piña colada protein smoothie
Prepare the basic recipe, omitting the orange juice and mango and adding
125ml (4fl.oz) coconut milk, 2 tablespoons coconut cream, and another
50g (2oz) chopped pineapple.

tropical protein smoothie
Prepare the basic recipe, omitting the orange juice and adding 225g (8oz)
Greek yoghurt (page 42) and 225g (8oz) tinned tropical fruit salad, drained.

strawberry protein smoothie
Prepare the basic recipe, omitting the pineapple and mango and adding
225g (8oz) fresh strawberries and 1 tablespoon strawberry jam.

variations

greek yoghurt

see base recipe page 42

honey yoghurt
Prepare the basic recipe. To serve, swirl 1 tablespoon of honey through each serving.

peach melba
Prepare the basic recipe. Put 3 or 4 slices of tinned or fresh peaches into individual dishes, then spoon about 125g (4oz) yoghurt over the peaches. Finish each serving with a few fresh raspberries.

cereal-enriched yoghurt
Prepare the basic recipe. Swirl 3 tablespoons Cherry–Berry Granola Crunch (page 65) per person through the yoghurt, just before serving.

strawberry yoghurt
Prepare the basic recipe. For each serving, crush 125g (4oz) fresh or frozen strawberries, mix with 1 tablespoon strawberry jam, and stir into the yoghurt. Add a special twist, if you wish, by serving the yoghurt in parfait glasses, layered alternating with a few extra fresh strawberries and some granola.

variations

apricot–oat smoothie

see base recipe page 44

peach–oat smoothie
Prepare the basic recipe, replacing the apricots with 225g (8oz) fresh or tinned peach slices. Omit the cinnamon.

non-dairy apricot–oat smoothie
Prepare the basic recipe, replacing the milk with oat (or soya) milk.

pineapple–oat smoothie
Prepare the basic recipe, omitting the apricots, ginger and cinnamon. Substitute 225g (8oz) sliced tinned or fresh pineapple and 2 tablespoons coconut cream.

raspberry–oat smoothie
Prepare the basic recipe, omitting the apricots and ginger. Substitute 225g (8oz) fresh raspberries and 1 tablespoon raspberry jam.

swiss muesli smoothie
Prepare the basic recipe, omitting the apricots and ginger. Add 225g (8oz) dried apples, 2 tablespoons wheatgerm and 1 teaspoon vanilla extract.

cereals & breakfast bars

Whether they're in a bar or a bowl, whole grain cereals are very good for our bodies. The fibre is necessary to keep your equilibrium in trim, and you will certainly notice a difference if you start incorporating whole grains into your daily breakfast.

two-in-one muesli

see variations page 74

Muesli cold or muesli hot with oats – this recipe gives you two ways to enjoy muesli.
You start by making a basic muesli mix (which is delicious by itself, perhaps topped with
a spoonful of yoghurt). When you want a hot cereal, you cook some of the mix with
milk and extra oats.

for the mueseli mix
350g (12oz) rolled oats
225g (8oz) whole wheat flakes (preferably
    toasted whole wheat flakes and
    flaxseed cereal)
225g (8oz) low-fat granola with raisins
85g (3oz) dried berries
30g (1oz) sultanas
3 tbsp sesame seeds

for the hot mueseli oatmeal
30g (1oz) chopped walnuts
475ml (16fl.oz) whole milk
225g (8oz) muesli mix
30g (1oz) rolled oats
2 tbsp sugar, or to taste
1 sliced banana, to serve

First make the muesli mix. In a large bowl, mix all the muesli ingredients, stirring until they
are combined well. This makes about 900g (2lb) muesli mix. Store in an airtight container.

To make the hot muesli oatmeal, in a medium saucepan, heat the milk and the muesli mix
with the extra rolled oats. Cook over medium heat, stirring constantly, until the milk has
been incorporated into the cereal. Add sugar, to taste. Serve immediately, with a sliced
banana on top.

Serves 2 (hot cereal)

honey muesli with raspberries & hazelnuts

see variations page 75

After making your own cereal, ready-made will never taste good enough again.

225g (8oz) rolled oats
50g (2oz) wheat germ
125ml (4fl.oz) freshly squeezed orange juice
50g (2oz) raisins

75g (3oz) hazelnuts, toasted
3 tbsp honey
fresh raspberries, to serve

In a large bowl, mix together the oats and wheat germ, stir in the orange juice and cover. Leave to soak overnight.

In the morning, add the raisins and hazelnuts. Drizzle with the honey. Spoon into bowls and sprinkle a few raspberries on top.

The muesli can be stored, without the raspberries, in an airtight container.

Serves 4–5

healthy cereal

see variations page 76

With all its nuts and seeds, this cereal has a wonderful texture and crunch.

275g (10oz) rolled oats
25g (1oz) sesame seeds
175g (6oz) chopped mixed nuts
75g (3oz) wheat germ
75g (3oz) unsweetened desiccated coconut
50g (2oz) sunflower seeds

125g (4oz) brown sugar
175ml (6fl.oz) sunflower or any light oil
175ml (6fl.oz) water
1/4 tsp salt
1 tsp vanilla extract

Preheat the oven to 175°C (350°F/Gas mark 4).

Combine the oats, sesame seeds, nuts, wheat germ, coconut, sunflower seeds and brown sugar in a large bowl. In a medium bowl, whisk together the oil, water, salt and vanilla extract. Stir the liquid mixture into the dry ingredients, mixing well. Spread mixture into a large roasting tin or over a baking tray and bake for 20–30 minutes, stirring occasionally, until crisp and golden.

Remove from oven and leave to cool, before storing in an airtight container.

Serves 6–8

great-for-you granola

see variations page 77

Do not be tempted to use ordinary barley in this recipe; it will be far too hard and crunchy. Just leave it out if it is not available.

800g (1¾lb) rolled oats
50g (2oz) wheat germ
50g (2oz) wheat bran
125g (4oz) sunflower seeds
275g (10oz) chopped mixed nuts
50g (2oz) quick-cooking barley (optional)
175g (6oz) brown sugar
175ml (6fl.oz) water
125ml (4fl.oz) sunflower or vegetable oil

50g (2oz) honey
50g (2oz) molasses or black treacle
pinch salt
1 tsp ground cinnamon
1 tsp ground nutmeg
1 tbsp vanilla extract
350g (12oz) mixed dried tropical fruit, such as
    pineapple, mango, figs and dates

Preheat the oven to 150°C (300°F/Gas mark 2). In a large bowl, mix together the oats, wheat germ, wheat bran, sunflower seeds, nuts and barley.

In a large saucepan, combine the brown sugar, water, oil, honey, molasses or treacle, salt, cinnamon, nutmeg and vanilla. Heat gently until the sugar is dissolved; do not boil. Cool slightly. Pour the syrup over the dry ingredients and stir well until thoroughly mixed. Spread mixture onto two baking trays in a thin layer and bake for about 45 minutes, stirring occasionally.

Remove from the oven and immediately add the dried fruit, stirring it in well. Leave to cool on the baking trays, then store in an airtight container.

Makes about 2.5kg (5½lb)

fruity sesame seed cereal

see variations page 78

There are countless combinations of oats, nuts and fruits to make your breakfast cereals enticing.

50ml (2fl.oz) sunflower oil or another light oil
50ml (2fl.oz) apple juice
4 tbsp honey
1 tsp ground cinnamon
275g (10oz) rolled oats

175g (6oz) chopped raw cashews
50g (2oz) flaked almonds
50g (2oz) sesame seeds
75g (3oz) raisins
75g (3oz) dried cranberries

Preheat the oven to 175°C (350°F/Gas mark 4). Put the oil, apple juice, honey and cinnamon in a large saucepan. Bring to a boil, stirring constantly. Stir in the oats, nuts and seeds, and combine well. Spread the mixture evenly over a baking tray or into a large roasting tin. Bake for about 20 minutes, stirring occasionally. Remove tin from the oven and stir in the raisins and cranberries. Leave to cool, then store in an airtight container.

Makes about 1.4kg (3lb)

cherry-berry granola crunch

see variations page 79

The aroma of this granola baking in the oven is so appetising you won't want to wait until morning!

2 tbsp sunflower or another light oil
125g (4oz) maple syrup
2 tbsp honey
1 tsp vanilla extract
400g (14oz) rolled oats

50g (2oz) sunflower seeds
50g (2oz) pumpkin seeds
4 tbsp sesame seeds
175g (6oz) mixed dried cherries and berries
75g (3oz) unsweetened desiccated coconut

Preheat the oven to 150°C (300°F/Gas mark 2). Mix the oil, maple syrup, honey and vanilla in a large bowl. Add the oats and sunflower, pumpkin and sesame seeds, and mix well. Spread the granola in a large roasting tin and bake for 15 minutes. Remove tin from oven, mix in the dried fruit and coconut and return to the oven for 10 more minutes. Remove from the oven and leave granola to cool in the tin. Store in an airtight container.

Makes about 1.1kg (2½lb)

power bars

see variations page 80

Having coffee in these bars gives a caffeine boost in the morning. They're great for people with no time to spare. Just wrap and go.

150g (5oz) chopped pecans
75g (3oz) flaked almonds
75g (3oz) unsweetened desiccated coconut
175g (6oz) rolled oats
175g (6oz) unsweetened rice cereal, such as
  Rice Krispies

225g (8oz) golden syrup
50g (2oz) brown sugar
pinch salt
2 tbsp freshly ground coffee
1 tsp vanilla extract

Preheat the oven to 175°C (350°F/Gas mark 4). Toast the nuts and coconut for 6–7 minutes on a baking tray, until the coconut is golden, stirring it once or twice. Watch carefully so that it does not burn. In a large bowl, combine the toasted nuts and coconut with the oats and rice cereal. Set aside.

Grease a 20cm (8in) square baking tin with a little vegetable oil. In a saucepan, heat together the syrup, brown sugar, salt, coffee and vanilla. Bring to the boil, stirring constantly. The mixture will thicken slightly as it cooks. Remove the pan from the heat and pour the syrup over the cereal mixture. Stir well to combine. Spread the mixture evenly in the greased baking tin, then let it cool to room temperature before cutting into bars.

Makes 9 bars

cranberry happy bars

see variations page 81

There is enough goodness in these bars to keep you on the go until lunch.

1 (400g/14oz) tin condensed milk
175g (6oz) rolled oats
75g (3oz) unsweetened desiccated coconut
50g (2oz) dried cranberries

25g (1oz) pumpkin seeds
25g (1oz) sunflower seeds
25g (1oz) sesame seeds
75g (3oz) chopped mixed nuts

Preheat the oven to 140°C (275°F/Gas mark 1) and grease a 23x33cm (9x13in) baking tin. In a large saucepan, gently warm the condensed milk. In a large bowl, combine all the other ingredients, then stir them into the warm condensed milk. Spread the mixture in the baking tin, pressing down to smooth the surface.

Bake for 1 hour, then remove tin from the oven. Cool in the tin for 15 minutes, then cut into 16 bars and leave to cool completely before serving.

Makes 16 bars

flapjacks

see variations page 82

These delicious crunchy bars are made with oats. They couldn't be easier to make.

125g (4oz) butter, plus extra for greasing
125g (4oz) sugar
4 tbsp golden syrup or dark golden syrup
175g (6oz) rolled oats

1 tsp baking powder
½ tsp salt
1 large egg, lightly beaten

Preheat the oven to 190°C (375°F/Gas mark 5). Grease a shallow 20x20cm (8x8in) baking tin and line it with baking paper. Put the butter, sugar and syrup into a medium saucepan and heat gently until the butter has melted. Stir in the remaining ingredients, and press the mixture into the baking tin. Bake for 20 minutes or until just golden at the edges. Remove from the oven and cool for 10 minutes.

Cut into bars in the tin and leave to sit until cold before removing.

Makes 16 bars

apple & almond bars

see variations page 83

Apples and almonds are a heavenly combination in this cakelike breakfast bar.

for the base and topping
225g (8oz) plain flour
½ tsp baking powder
225g (8oz) butter
125g (4oz) sugar
½ tsp salt
50g (2oz) flaked almonds
2 egg yolks, lightly beaten
1 tsp almond extract

for the filling
175g (6oz) sugar
25g (1oz) flour
1 tsp ground cinnamon
½ tsp. ground nutmeg
4 medium cooking apples,
    peeled, cored and flaked

for the icing
1 tbsp milk
½ tsp. almond extract
75g (3oz) sifted icing sugar

Preheat the oven to 175°C (350°F/Gas mark 4). For the base and topping, sift the flour and baking powder into a large bowl. Cut in the butter, using a pastry blender or your hands, until the pieces are the size of small peas. Add the sugar, salt and almonds. Using a fork, stir in the egg yolks and the almond extract. Press half of the crumb mixture into the bottom of an ungreased 23x33cm (9x13in) baking tin. Set aside.

In another bowl, make the filling. Stir together the sugar, flour, cinnamon and nutmeg. Add the apples and toss to combine. Arrange evenly over the crumb mixture and sprinkle the remaining crumb mixture evenly over the top. Bake for about 35 minutes, until the top is golden. Cool in the tin on a wire rack.

For the icing, stir together the milk, almond extract and sugar in a small bowl. Drizzle over the top, leave to set, then cut into bars.
Makes 24

variations

two-in-one muesli

see base recipe page 57

cold muesli mix & berries
Prepare the basic muesli mix and serve it cold, mixed with cold milk, and topped with fresh berries.

cold muesli mix with macadamia nuts & coconut
Prepare the basic muesli mix, replacing the walnuts with chopped macadamia nuts and adding 45g (1½oz) unsweetened desiccated coconut.

hot muesli oatmeal with pecans & pineapple
Prepare the basic muesli mix, replacing the walnuts with pecans and adding 60g (2oz) dried chopped pineapple.

hot muesli oatmeal with spices & maple syrup
Prepare the basic muesli mix, adding ½ teaspoon mixed spice with the extra rolled oats. Serve with the sliced banana and a generous swirl of maple syrup.

honey muesli with raspberries & hazelnuts

see base recipe page 58

honey muesli with figs & almonds
Prepare the basic recipe, replacing the hazelnuts with flaked almonds and the raisins with 75g (3oz) dried figs.

honey muesli with coconut & chocolate
Prepare the basic recipe, omitting the raspberries. Add 50g (2oz) unsweetened desiccated coconut to the cereal mix and stir in 50g (2oz) plain chocolate chips just before serving.

honey muesli with apricot & ginger
Prepare the basic recipe, omitting the raspberries. Add 2 teaspoons ground ginger to the cereal mixture. Just before serving, sprinkle cereal with 125g (4oz) chopped fresh, tinned or dried apricots.

honey muesli with pears & cranberries
Prepare the basic recipe, replacing the raisins with 50g (2oz) dried cranberries and the raspberries with 125g (4oz) peeled, cored, and sliced pears.

honey muesli with pineapple & macadamia nuts
Prepare the basic recipe, replacing the raisins with 50g (2oz) chopped macadamia nuts and the raspberries with 50g (2oz) dried pineapple pieces.

variations

healthy cereal

see base recipe page 61

berry healthy cereal
Prepare the basic recipe, adding 50g (2oz) dried berries (preferably a medley of berries) to the cereal when it is fresh from the oven. Stir in well.

apple healthy cereal
Prepare the basic recipe, omitting the coconut. Add 2 teaspoons ground cinnamon to the cereal mix with the nuts. Add 75g (3oz) dried apple slices to the cereal when it is fresh from the oven. Stir them in well.

very seedy healthy cereal
Prepare the basic recipe, adding 25g (1oz) flaxseeds and 25g (1oz) pumpkin seeds to the cereal mix with the other seeds.

malted cereal
Prepare the basic recipe, adding 25g (1oz) malted drink powder to the cereal mix with the oats.

variations

great-for-you granola

see base recipe page 62

great-for-you granola with flaxseed
Prepare the basic recipe, adding 25g (1oz) ground flaxseed.

christmas granola
Prepare the basic recipe, omitting the barley. Replace the tropical fruit with
50g (2oz) each of glacé cherries, dark raisins and currants. Add 1 tablespoon dried
mixed peel, if desired. Add an extra 1 teaspoon each of cinnamon and nutmeg.

autumnal granola
Prepare the basic recipe, replacing the tropical dried fruit with 50g (2oz) each of
dried apples, dried chopped apricots, and dried cranberries.

gingerbread granola
Prepare the basic recipe, adding 3 teaspoons ground ginger with the other spices.

great-for-you granola bars
Prepare the basic recipe. In a large saucepan, heat 175g (6oz) butter and mix
in the granola and 2 beaten eggs. Mix well and put into a greased 23x33cm
(9x13in) metal baking tin. Bake at 175°C (350°F/Gas mark 4) for about 30 minutes,
until golden.

variations

fruity sesame seed cereal

see base recipe page 64

walnut & banana sesame seed cereal
Prepare the basic recipe, replacing the cashews and raisins with 125g (4oz) chopped walnuts and 50g (2oz) dried banana chips.

currant & raisin sesame seed cereal
Prepare the basic recipe, replacing the raisins and cranberries with 75g (3oz) currants and 75g (3oz) sultanas.

hazelnut & pecan sesame seed cereal
Prepare the basic recipe, replacing the cashews and flaked almonds with 50g (2oz) hazelnuts and 50g (2oz) chopped pecans.

tropical sesame seed cereal
Prepare the basic recipe, replacing the raisins and cranberries with 50g (2oz) dried chopped apricots and 75g (3oz) dried chopped dates.

crunchy banana, walnut & sesame seed cereal
Prepare the basic recipe, omitting the cashews. Add 25g (1oz) dried banana chips and 125g (4oz) chopped walnuts.

cherry–berry granola crunch

see base recipe page 65

heart-happy crunchy granola
Prepare the basic recipe, replacing the sunflower oil with 2 tablespoons vegetable oil and adding 50g (2oz) chopped walnuts and 25g (1oz) dried banana chips.

pecan & hazelnut crunchy granola
Prepare the basic recipe, adding 50g (2oz) chopped pecans and 50g (2oz) chopped hazelnuts.

chocolate macadamia nut granola
Prepare the basic recipe, omitting the cherries and berries. Add 50g (2oz) chopped macadamia nuts to the granola before cooking. When the granola has cooled, stir in 125g (4oz) plain chocolate chips.

date & walnut crunchy granola
Prepare the basic recipe, omitting the cherries and berries. Add 50g (2oz) chopped walnuts to the granola before cooking, and 75g (3oz) chopped dried dates in the last 10 minutes of cooking.

variations

power bars

see base recipe page 66

maple power bars
Prepare the basic recipe, replacing the golden syrup with maple syrup.

high-fiber power bars
Prepare the basic recipe, adding 25g (1oz) wheat bran to the cereal mix with the toasted nuts and coconut.

chocolate chip power bars
Prepare the basic recipe, adding 25g (1oz) plain chocolate chips to the cereal mix with the toasted nuts and coconut.

tropical power bars
Prepare the basic recipe, adding 25g (1oz) dried tropical fruits to the cereal mix with the toasted nuts and coconut.

cranberry happy bars

see base recipe page 68

raisin happy bars
Prepare the basic recipe, replacing the cranberries with 50g (2oz) raisins.

pineapple & macadamia happy bars
Prepare the basic recipe, replacing the cranberries with 50g (2oz) chopped candied pineapple and the chopped mixed nuts with chopped macadamia nuts.

date & pecan happy bars
Prepare the basic recipe, replacing the cranberries with chopped dates and the mixed nuts with 75g (3oz) chopped pecans.

berry happy bars
Prepare the basic recipe, replacing the cranberries with 50g (2oz) mixed dried berries and cherries.

variations

flapjacks

see base recipe page 71

coconut flapjacks
Prepare the basic recipe, adding 75g (3oz) unsweetened desiccated coconut.

almond flapjacks
Prepare the basic recipe, adding 25g (1oz) ground almonds and 25g (1oz) flaked almonds.

cherry flapjacks
Prepare the basic recipe, adding 25g (1oz) glacé cherries and 1 teaspoon vanilla extract.

ginger flapjacks
Prepare the basic recipe, adding 25g (1oz) crystallised ginger and 1 teaspoon ground ginger.

apricot & raisin flapjacks
Prepare the basic recipe, adding 25g (1oz) chopped dried apricots and 25g (1oz) raisins.

apple & almond bars

see base recipe page 72

apricot & almond bars
Prepare the basic recipe, replacing the apples with 450g (1lb) sliced apricots.
Instead of the basic icing, use an orange icing, made by blending together
in a small bowl 50g (2oz) icing sugar, pinch of ground cinnamon, and
3–4 teaspoons orange juice (enough to make a drizzling consistency).

cherry & almond bars
Prepare the basic recipe, replacing the apples with 450g (1lb) fresh or tinned
pitted cherries.

raspberry, apple & almond bars
Prepare the basic recipe, adding 50g (2oz) fresh raspberries to the apples
in the filling. Instead of the basic icing, mix 125g (4oz) sifted icing sugar,
1 tablespoon melted butter, 1 teaspoon vanilla extract, ½ teaspoon ground
cinnamon, and 2–3 teaspoons milk (enough to make a drizzling consistency).

blackberry, apple & almond bars
Prepare the basic recipe, adding 50g (2oz) fresh blackberries to the apples
in the filling.

breads

If you have never made bread before, now is the time to start. Not only does it smell divine as it bakes, the taste is heavenly. Besides, you can control what goes into it, and make it as healthy or indulgent as you want.

rustic loaf

see variations page 106

This is a quick mix basic bread loaf, an easy introduction to home bread making.

450g (1lb) white bread flour
2 tsp salt
4 tbsp olive oil

1 envelope active dried yeast
300ml (10fl.oz) lukewarm water

Mix all the ingredients together in a large bowl, taking care not to add the yeast on top of the salt. Bring the dough together with your hands. If it feels a little sticky, add more flour, and if it fails to come together properly, add a little more water. Knead well with your hands and knuckles until the dough is soft, smooth and elastic. Alternatively, knead the dough for 5 minutes with the dough hook of your mixer.

Put the dough into a greased bowl, then turn the dough so that the top is greased as well. This will stop a crust from forming while the dough rises. Cover the bowl with clingfilm and leave in a warm place until the dough has doubled in size.

Turn onto a lightly floured surface and knock back slightly. Mould into a round, slightly oval shape and place on a baking tray lined with baking paper. Cut a few diagonal slashes across the top and dust with white flour. Leave to rise again for another hour.

Heat the oven to 220°C (425°F/Gas mark 7). Bake the loaf for 30 minutes until golden brown. Remove from the oven. Tap the bottom of the loaf; if it sounds hollow, it is cooked. If not, return to the oven for another few minutes. Cool on a wire rack.

Makes 1 loaf

no-yeast soda bread

see variations page 107

This bread is excellent with cheese. It is quickly made and should be eaten very fresh, as it does not keep well.

385g (13½ oz) plain flour
2 level tsp bicarbonate of soda
2 level tsp cream of tartar
1 level tsp salt

2 tbsp white vegetable fat
1-2 tsp sugar (optional)
250ml (9fl.oz) buttermilk
2 tbsp whole milk

Preheat the oven to 200°C (400°F/Gas mark 6). Sift the flour, bicarbonate of soda, cream of tartar and salt into a large bowl. Cut the vegetable fat up and rub it into the dry ingredients with your fingertips until the mixture resembles fine breadcrumbs. Mix in the sugar, if using. Make a well in the centre of the flour, add the buttermilk and milk and mix to a soft but manageable dough, working it with a round-bladed knife.

Turn the dough onto a lightly floured surface, knead it lightly, and shape it into a 18cm (7in) round. Flatten it slightly with your hand. With the back of a knife, make a large cross across the loaf, set it on a floured baking tray and bake in the centre of the oven for about 30 minutes. Cool on a wire rack and serve.

Makes 1 loaf

multigrain bread

see variations page 108

Baking your own wholemeal bread can give you a better, healthier and tastier loaf, and is so easy to do, especially if you have a mixer with a dough hook.

1 tsp sugar
175ml (6fl.oz) lukewarm water
1 envelope active dried yeast
175g (6oz) white bread flour
200g (7oz) wholewheat flour
25g (1oz) wheatgerm
25g (1oz) oat bran

1½ tsp salt
75ml (3fl.oz) milk
3 tbsp honey
3 tbsp olive oil
1 tsp salt mixed with 2 tbsp water
cracked wheat or rolled oats, for sprinkling top

Dissolve the sugar in the warm water and sprinkle the yeast on top. Set aside until frothy, about 10-15 minutes. In a large bowl, mix the flours, wheatgerm, oat bran and salt. Make a well in the centre and pour in the yeast liquid and the milk, honey and olive oil. Knead with your hands and knuckles to make a smooth, soft dough. Alternatively, knead in mixer with a dough hook for 5 minutes. Shape the dough into a ball, and place on a greased baking tray. Brush top with salt and water mixture, and sprinkle with cracked wheat or oats. Cover with clingfilm, and leave in a warm place until the dough has doubled in size, about 1½ hours.

Meanwhile preheat the oven to 200°C (400°F/Gas mark 6). When the dough is ready, bake the bread for about 30 minutes, until nicely browned. Turn out and cool on a wire rack.

Makes 1 loaf

raisin bread

see variations page 109

This bread is delicious sliced and spread with butter. Kids love it!

385g (13½ oz) plain flour
1 envelope active dried yeast
1 tsp sugar
125ml (4fl.oz) lukewarm milk
30g (1½oz) unsalted butter
125g (4oz) brown sugar

¾ tsp salt
1 tsp ground cinnamon
1 tsp ground nutmeg
175g (6oz) raisins
1 large egg, lightly beaten

Measure 50g (2oz) flour into a bowl. Add the yeast, sugar and warm milk, mixing well. Set aside until frothy, about 20 minutes. Using a pastry blender or your fingertips, cut the butter into the remaining flour. Mix in the brown sugar, salt, spices and raisins. Add the egg and the yeast liquid and combine well. Knead with your hands and knuckles on a lightly floured surface until you have a soft, smooth and elastic dough. Alternatively knead the dough in a mixer with a dough hook for 5 minutes. Place the dough in a greased bowl, turning so that the dough is evenly coated, cover with clingfilm and leave at room temperature until doubled in size.

Turn dough out onto a lightly floured surface and knock back. Knead again and shape to fit a greased 450g (1lb) loaf tin. Place tin in a greased plastic bag, tie bag loosely and set aside to let rise to about 2.5cm (1in) above the top of the loaf tin. Preheat the oven to 175°C (350°F/Gas mark 4). Brush with beaten egg and bake the loaf for 30 minutes or until golden brown. Leave to cool in the tin for 5 minutes, then turn out and cool on a wire rack.

Makes 1 loaf

brötchen

see variations page 110

You could serve these traditional German white rolls as part of a continental breakfast, with lots of butter and strawberry jam. They also make great dinner rolls.

1 tsp sugar	650g (1½ lb) white bread flour
350ml (12fl.oz) lukewarm water	1 tsp salt
1 envelope active dried yeast	25g (1oz) white vegetable fat

Prepare the yeast liquid by dissolving the sugar in the water and sprinkling the yeast on top. Leave until frothy, about 10-15 minutes. Sift the flour and salt into a large bowl, then, using a pastry blender or your fingertips, cut in the vegetable fat until it resembles fine breadcrumbs. Add the yeast liquid and work to a firm dough. Turn onto a lightly floured surface and knead thoroughly with your hands and knuckles, until you have a soft, smooth and elastic dough. Alternatively knead the dough for 5 minutes in a mixer with a dough hook. Put the dough into a greased bowl, turning to coat it all over, and cover with clingfilm. Leave to rise in a warm place until doubled in size.

Turn the dough onto a lightly floured surface and knock back slightly. Divide dough evenly into 18 pieces and shape them into balls. Press down hard at first with the palm of your hand, then ease up. Place the brötchen about 2.5cm (1in) apart on baking trays. Cover with lightly oiled clingfilm and leave for about 30 minutes at room temperature. Preheat the oven to 230°C (450°F/Gas mark 8). Remove the clingfilm and bake the brötchen for 15–20 minutes. Remove from the oven and cool on a wire rack. Although these are terrific served the same day, they can be kept a few days and rewarmed before serving.

Makes 18

italian herb bread

see variations page 111

This bread is especially delicious when sliced and buttered to accompany an omelette.

175ml (6fl.oz) lukewarm water
125ml (4fl.oz) lukewarm milk
1½ tsp sugar
1 envelope active dried yeast
3 tbsp olive oil
1 clove garlic, crushed

2 tsp dried basil
1 tsp dried oregano
1 tsp dried thyme
650g (1½lb) white bread flour, plus extra
   to sprinkle
1 tsp salt

Mix the warm water and warm milk in a small bowl, then add the sugar to dissolve. Sprinkle the yeast on top. Set aside until frothy, about 10-15 minutes. In a small frying pan set over a low heat, warm the oil and sauté the garlic and herbs together gently. Do not heat the garlic too much or it will be bitter. Cool.

In a large bowl, mix the flour and the salt. Make a well in the centre and add the yeast liquid and the garlic and herb mixture. Work to a soft dough. Turn out onto a lightly floured surface and knead, using your hands and knuckles, until you have a soft, smooth, and elastic dough. Alternatively, knead for 5 minutes in a mixer with a dough hook. Place the dough in a greased bowl and turn so that the dough is greased all over. Cover and leave to rise in a warm place until doubled. Turn the dough out onto a lightly floured surface, knock back, and knead a little more. Form dough into an oval about 20–25cm (8–10in) long and place it on a floured baking tray. Cover and let rise again until doubled. Preheat the oven to 200°C (400°F/ Gas mark 6). Remove cover and bake the bread for about 30 minutes. Cool on a wire rack. Sprinkle with flour to serve.

Makes 1 loaf

pumpkin swirl bread

see variations page 112

This wonderful breakfast bread is even more delicious when made into French toast.

butter, for greasing
1 tsp sugar
50ml (2fl.oz) lukewarm water
1 envelope active dried yeast
400g (14oz) white bread flour
1 tsp ground cinnamon
1 tsp ground ginger
¼ tsp ground cloves
1 tsp ground allspice
1 tsp salt

3 tbsp sunflower oil, plus extra for greasing
50ml (2fl.oz) lukewarm milk
200g (7oz) pumpkin purée
175g (6oz) brown sugar
75g (3oz) raisins
75g (3oz) chopped walnuts
25g (1oz) butter, melted
2 tbsp sugar mixed with 2 tsp ground cinnamon
1 egg, beaten with a little milk

Grease a 900g (2lb) loaf tin with butter. Prepare the yeast liquid by dissolving sugar in warm water and sprinkling yeast on top. Leave until frothy, about 10-15 minutes. In a large bowl, combine the flour with the spices and salt. In a separate bowl, mix 3 tablespoons oil, warm milk, pumpkin purée and brown sugar. Add to the flour with yeast liquid, then work the ingredients into a soft dough. Turn out onto a lightly floured surface and knead, using your hands and knuckles, until you have a soft, smooth and elastic dough. If the dough feels too sticky, add a little flour, and if it fails to come together properly, add a little water. Alternatively, knead the dough for 5 minutes in a mixer with a dough hook.

Roll dough out to a thick circle. Spread raisins and walnuts over dough and carefully knead them in. Shape dough into a ball and put it into a greased bowl, turning it so that all the dough is greased. Cover and leave until doubled.

Turn dough out onto a lightly floured surface and knock back. Knead again and roll out to a 20x30cm (8x12in) oblong, 1cm (½in) thick. Brush dough with melted butter and sprinkle evenly with cinnamon sugar. Roll dough very tightly like a swiss roll, and pull it out at the corners as it shrinks a little. When you have finished rolling, seal edges by pinching them together.

Place roll, seam-side down, in the buttered loaf tin, cover, and leave to rise again until doubled. Meanwhile, preheat the oven to 175°C (350°F/Gas mark 4). Remove cover, brush with a glaze of beaten egg and milk, and bake for about 40 minutes. Leave to cool for 10 minutes in the tin before turning out to cool completely on a wire rack.
Makes 1 loaf

brioches

see variations page 113

Brioche is a slightly sweet French bread, highly enriched with butter and eggs. You will need 12 x 8cm (3in) fluted brioche tins for these little individual rolls.

250g (9oz) white bread flour
½ level tsp salt
1 tbsp. sugar
3 tbsp lukewarm water

1 envelope active dried yeast
2 eggs, beaten, plus extra for brushing
25g (1oz) butter, melted
oil, for brushing

Sift flour and salt into a bowl. Dissolve sugar in warm water and sprinkle yeast on top. Leave for a few minutes until frothy, then stir it, together with beaten eggs and melted butter, into flour and salt. Using a wooden spoon, beat dough until it leaves the sides of the bowl clean, then turn it out onto a lightly floured surface and knead for 5 minutes. Alternatively, knead dough for 5 minutes in a mixer with a dough hook. Put dough in an oiled bowl, turn it around, cover with clingfilm, and leave at room temperature to rise until doubled. Turn dough out onto a lightly floured surface and knead until smooth. Shape dough into a long sausage and cut into 12 equal pieces.

Brush brioche pans with oil and shape ¾ of each piece of dough into a ball. Place it in the tin. Using a floured finger, press a hole in the centre of the dough as far as the base of the tin. Shape remaining piece of dough into a ball and insert it in the hole. Press lightly with fingertip to unite the two pieces of dough. Repeat with remaining brioches, set tins on a baking tray, cover loosely with clingfilm and leave to rise until the dough is puffy and just below the tops of the tins. Preheat the oven to 230°C (450°F/Gas mark 8). Remove clingfilm, brush the tops of the brioches with egg and bake for 10 minutes, or until golden brown.
Makes 12

all-day breakfast bread

see variations page 114

Everything you want for breakfast wrapped up in a warm loaf of bread.

butter, for greasing
1 tsp sugar
300ml (10fl.oz) lukewarm water
1 envelope active dried yeast
450g (1lb) white bread flour
1 tsp salt

for the filling
12g (½oz) butter, melted
4 rashers cooked, crisp bacon
4 cooked chipolatas, sliced
2 hard-boiled eggs, chopped

Grease a 900g (2lb) loaf tin with butter. Dissolve sugar in warm water and sprinkle yeast on top. Leave until frothy, about 10-15 minutes. In a large bowl, mix flour and salt. Make a well in the centre and pour in yeast liquid. Work to a soft dough. Turn out onto a lightly floured surface and knead with your hands and knuckles until the dough is soft, smooth and elastic. Alternatively, knead dough in a mixer with a dough hook. Put dough into a greased bowl, turning it so that it is greased all over, cover and leave to rise at room temperature until doubled in size.

Turn the dough out onto a lightly floured surface and roll out to a 20x30cm (8x12in) rectangle. For the filling, brush with melted butter, then sprinkle bacon, sausage and eggs evenly over the top. Roll dough up like a swiss roll and seal the edges together by pinching with your fingers. Put dough into greased loaf tin, seam-side down, cover and leave to rise until doubled. Preheat oven to 220°C (425°F/Gas mark 7). Remove the cover and bake bread for about 30 minutes. Leave to cool in the tin for 10 minutes, then turn out and cool on a wire rack.

Makes 1 loaf

banana cranberry loaf

see variations page 115

Slightly sweet and flavoured with cranberries, this loaf is terrific toasted with butter.

75g (3oz) unsalted butter, softened, plus extra
    for greasing
125g (4oz) caster sugar
175g (6oz) plain flour
25g (1oz) wholewheat flour
½ tsp salt

2 tsp baking powder
¼ tsp bicarbonate of soda
3 medium-size bananas (2 very ripe)
50ml (2fl.oz) buttermilk
2 large eggs, beaten
75g (3oz) chopped dried cranberries

Preheat the oven to 175°C (350°F/Gas mark 4). Grease a 450g (1lb) loaf tin and dust with flour. In a large bowl, beat the butter and the sugar together until creamy. In a separate bowl, combine the dry ingredients. In yet another bowl, mash the 2 ripe bananas with the buttermilk.

Add the beaten eggs gradually to the creamed butter and sugar. Add the mashed bananas and the dry ingredients and mix lightly until combined. Do not overmix. Slice the third banana and add it to the batter with the cranberries, stirring lightly until just combined. Pour the batter into the loaf tin and bake in the middle of the oven for about 40 minutes or until a toothpick inserted into the centre comes out clean. Leave in the tin for 10 minutes, then turn out and cool on a wire rack.

Makes 1 loaf

monkey bread

see variations page 116

This is a sweet pull-apart bread, delicious when at room temperature, delectable when warm. Traditionally monkey bread is baked in a tube pan, but a round dish is fine.

butter, for greasing
1 tsp sugar
300ml (10fl.oz) lukewarm milk
1 envelope active dried yeast
450g (1lb) white bread flour
1 tsp salt
1 tbsp grated orange zest

for glaze & coating
40g (2½oz) butter
3 tbsp orange juice
50g (2oz) brown sugar
1 tbsp ground cinnamon
350g (12oz) sugar

Grease a large semicircular tin, round casserole dish or cake tin. Dissolve sugar in warm milk, then sprinkle yeast over top. Set aside until frothy, 10-15 minutes. In a large bowl, mix flour, salt and orange zest. Make a well in the centre and pour in yeast liquid. Work to a soft dough, turn out onto a lightly floured surface, and knead until it is soft, smooth and elastic (or use a mixer). Place dough in a greased bowl, turning to grease all over, cover and leave to rise in a warm place until doubled in size.

To make glaze, over a medium heat, melt the butter in a small saucepan with orange juice, then add brown sugar and stir to dissolve. In a small bowl, mix cinnamon and sugar. Turn dough onto a lightly floured surface, knock back, and break into about 30–35 pieces. Roll into balls. Dip each ball into the glaze and then roll in the cinnamon sugar. Start layering the balls in the tube pan, leaving room on the bottom layer for the balls to expand as they rise. They should be close, but not touching. On each successive layer, place balls so that they overlap empty spaces underneath. When you have used up all the balls, cover and leave to

rise until doubled in size. Meanwhile, preheat the oven to 175°C (350°F/Gas mark 4). Remove cover from bread, pour any remaining glaze over the top and sprinkle on remaining cinnamon sugar. Bake for about 25–30 minutes, until lightly browned. Invert bread onto a serving plate, being careful of hot syrup. Cool slightly, then serve.

Makes 1

classic french baguette

see variations page 117

This bread will become stale within one day, so it's best eaten as soon as possible.

1 tsp sugar	350g (12oz) white bread flour
225ml (8fl.oz) lukewarm water	1 tsp salt
1 envelope active dried yeast	

Dissolve the sugar in the warm water, then sprinkle the yeast on top. Leave until frothy, about 10-15 minutes. In a large bowl, mix flour and salt. Make a well in the centre, pour in yeast liquid and work to a soft dough. Turn onto a lightly floured surface and knead until you have a soft, smooth and elastic dough. Alternatively, knead for 5 minutes in a mixer with a dough hook. Place dough in a greased bowl, turning it so that it is greased all over, cover and leave to rise at room temperature until doubled.

Turn dough out onto a lightly floured surface and knock back lightly. Roll out to a 40x30cm (16x12in) rectangle, and then cut in half to make two 20x30cm (8x12in) rectangles. Roll up each piece tightly from the longer side, pushing out any air bubbles as you go. Pinch together the dough along the seam and at each end. Place seam-side down, 8cm (3in) apart, on a greased baking tray and make deep gashes diagonally across each loaf every 5cm (2in). Cover and leave to rise until doubled in size.

Meanwhile, preheat the oven to 220°C (425°F/Gas mark 7). Remove cover from the loaves and bake for 10-12 minutes or until golden brown. Cool on a wire rack.

Makes 2 loaves

variations

rustic loaf

see base recipe page 85

tomato & olive loaf
Prepare basic recipe, adding 125g (4oz) pitted and chopped black olives
and 125g (4oz) drained and chopped sun-dried tomatoes during the
first kneading.

apple bran bread
Prepare basic recipe, replacing 25g (1oz) bread flour with 25g (1oz)
wholemeal flour. Add 1 tablespoon wheat bran; 2 apples, peeled, cored
and grated; 1 tablespoon sugar; and 1 teaspoon ground cinnamon.

basil & parmesan loaf
Prepare basic recipe, adding 1 tablespoon dried basil and 2 tablespoons
finely grated Parmesan cheese to the flour.

foccacia
Prepare basic recipe. After the first rising, roll dough into a round about
1cm (½in) thick. Place on baking tray and sprinkle with 2 teaspoons dried
rosemary and 2 minced garlic cloves. Poke shallow indentations all over
dough with your fingertips, then pour 1 tablespoon olive oil on top so it
pools in indentations. Bake for about 20 minutes, until lightly browned.

variations

no-yeast soda bread

see base recipe page 86

soda bread with onion & dill
Prepare the basic recipe, adding 1 tablespoon dry minced onion and
1 tablespoon dried dill to the flour before mixing.

soda bread with cheese & mustard
Prepare the basic recipe, adding 50g (2oz) grated Cheddar cheese and
2 teaspoons dry mustard to the flour before mixing.

soda bread with sweet red pepper & sage
Prepare the basic recipe, adding 50g (2oz) finely chopped roasted red peppers
and 1 tablespoon (or less, if desired) dried sage to the flour before mixing.

soda bread with fruit & oats
Prepare the basic recipe, replacing 2 tablespoons of the flour with
2 tablespoons rolled oats and adding 125g (4oz) chopped dried fruit
and 1 tablespoon ground cinnamon.

multigrain bread

see base recipe page 89

multigrain bread with brown sugar & pecans
Prepare the basic recipe, omitting the honey. Add 4 tablespoons brown sugar and 50g (2oz) chopped pecans to the flours before mixing.

multigrain bread with bulgur wheat
Prepare the basic recipe, adding 3 tablespoons bulgur wheat to the flours before mixing.

multigrain & orange bread
Prepare the basic recipe, replacing the milk with buttermilk. Add 2 tablespoons grated orange zest to the flours before mixing.

multigrain bread with garlic & rosemary
Prepare the basic recipe, omitting the honey. Add 1 minced garlic clove and 1 tablespoon dried rosemary to the flours before mixing.

multigrain bread with sunflower seeds
Prepare the basic recipe, adding 3 tablespoons sunflower seeds to the flours before mixing.

raisin bread

see base recipe page 90

raisin bread with coconut & banana
Prepare the basic recipe, adding 25g (1oz) unsweetened desiccated coconut and
1 mashed banana.

raisin bread with mango & macadamia nuts
Prepare the basic recipe, omitting 50g (2oz) raisins and adding 50g (2oz) chopped
fresh mango and 50g (2oz) chopped macadamia nuts.

raisin bread with orange & almond
Prepare the basic recipe, omitting 50g (2oz) raisins and adding 1 tablespoon finely
chopped orange zest and 50g (2oz) chopped almonds.

cranberry–raisin bread
Prepare the basic recipe, replacing 50g (2oz) raisins with 50g (2oz) dried cranberries.

cherry–raisin bread
Prepare the basic recipe, replacing 50g (2oz) raisins with 50g (2oz) dried cherries.

variations

brötchen

see base recipe page 92

poppy seed brötchen
Prepare the basic recipe, adding 2 tablespoons poppy seeds.

brötchen with flaxseeds
Prepare the basic recipe, omitting 25g (1oz) white bread flour, and
substituting 25g (1oz) flaxseed meal and 2 teaspoons malt powder
(if available). Sprinkle a few flaxseeds on top of the rolls before baking,
pressing them into the dough slightly.

brötchen with wholemeal flour
Prepare the basic recipe, replacing 150g (5oz) white bread flour with
150g (5oz) wholemeal flour.

brötchen with bran & sesame seeds
Prepare the basic recipe, omitting 25g (1oz) white bread flour and adding
2 tablespoons wheat bran and 2 tablespoons sesame seeds.

brötchen with garlic pepper
Prepare the basic recipe, adding 1 finely chopped garlic clove and
1 tablespoon garlic pepper to the flour before mixing.

italian herb bread

see base recipe page 93

italian herb bread with lemon & poppy seed
Prepare the basic recipe, omitting the oil, garlic and herbs. Add 1 tablespoon grated lemon zest and 1 tablespoon poppy seeds.

italian herb bread with pesto swirl
Prepare the basic recipe, omitting the herbs. After the first rising, roll the dough out to a 20x35cm (8x14in) rectangle. Spread 4 tablespoons pesto over the dough and roll it up like a swiss roll. Put into a greased baking tin for the second rising until doubled in size. Bake for about 30 minutes.

italian cardamom & herb bread
Prepare the basic recipe, adding 2 teaspoons ground cardamom to the other herbs.

italian herb bread with onion & oregano
Prepare the basic recipe, omitting the thyme and adding 1 tablespoon dried onion flakes and an extra 2 teaspoons oregano.

italian herb bread with pumpkin seeds
Prepare the basic recipe, omitting the garlic and adding 25g (1oz) pumpkin seeds.

variations

pumpkin swirl bread

see base recipe page 94

pumpkin swirl bread with trail mix
Prepare the basic recipe, replacing the cinnamon sugar in the swirl with
3 tablespoons trail mix.

pumpkin, cranberry & orange swirl bread
Prepare the basic recipe, replacing the raisins with 50g (2oz) dried
cranberries and 1 tablespoon grated orange zest.

pumpkin, apple & ginger swirl bread
Prepare the basic recipe, replacing the raisins with 2 peeled, cored and finely
grated apples. Add an extra teaspoon of ground ginger to the ingredients.

pumpkin, pecan & sultana swirl bread
Prepare the basic recipe, replacing the raisins and walnuts with sultanas and
chopped pecans.

pumpkin, cherry & almond swirl bread
Prepare the basic recipe, replacing the raisins and walnuts with dried cherries
and chopped almonds.

variations

brioches

see base recipe page 97

brioches with raisins
Prepare the basic recipe, adding 125g (4oz) raisins to the flour with the water and butter.

brioches with chocolate
Prepare the basic recipe, adding 50g (2oz) chocolate chips to the flour with the water and butter.

brioches with cinnamon
Prepare the basic recipe, adding 2 teaspoons ground cinnamon to the flour with the yeast mixture.

brioches with nutmeg
Prepare the basic recipe, adding 1 teaspoon ground nutmeg to the flour with the yeast mixture.

brioches with almonds
Prepare the basic recipe. After brushing the brioches with beaten egg, scatter a few flaked almonds over the top of each one.

variations

all-day breakfast bread

see base recipe page 98

maple & pecan breakfast bread
Prepare the basic recipe, omitting the bacon, sausage and eggs. Add
2 tablespoons melted butter and 2 tablespoons maple syrup to the flour
mixture. Sprinkle 50g (2oz) chopped pecans and 50g (2oz) brown sugar on
the dough before rolling up.

cheese & black olive breakfast bread
Prepare the basic recipe, omitting the bacon, sausage and eggs.
Substitute 50g (2oz) pitted and chopped black olives and 50g (2oz)
grated Cheddar cheese.

ham & mushroom breakfast bread
Prepare the basic recipe, omitting the bacon, sausage and eggs. Substitute
125g (4oz) chopped ham and 25g (1oz) chopped lightly fried mushrooms.

cheese & onion breakfast bread
Prepare the basic recipe, omitting the sausage and eggs. Substitute 25g (1oz)
grated Cheddar cheese and 25g (1oz) chopped lightly fried onion.

variations

banana cranberry loaf

see base recipe page 101

banana, cherry & macadamia loaf
Prepare the basic recipe, omitting the cranberries and substituting 25g (1oz) chopped glacé cherries and 25g (1oz) chopped macadamia nuts.

banana, fig & almond loaf
Prepare the basic recipe, omitting the cranberries and substituting 25g (1oz) chopped dried figs and 25g (1oz) chopped almonds.

banana, date & walnut loaf
Prepare the basic recipe, omitting the cranberries and substituting 25g (1oz) chopped dates and 25g (1oz) chopped walnuts.

tropical pineapple & coconut loaf
Prepare the basic recipe, omitting the cranberries and substituting 25g (1oz) chopped candied pineapple and 25g (1oz) unsweetened desiccated coconut.

banana cranberry loaf with ginger
Prepare the basic recipe, adding 2 teaspoons ground ginger.

variations

monkey bread

see base recipe page 102

monkey bread with maple cinnamon sugar
Prepare the basic recipe, omitting the orange zest and orange juice, and 50g (2oz) of the white sugar, and substituting 3 tablespoons maple syrup.

monkey bread with garlic & herbs
Prepare the basic recipe, replacing orange zest with 1 minced garlic clove. Omit orange juice, both sugars and cinnamon in the glaze. Instead, mix melted butter with 2 minced garlic cloves and ½ teaspoon each of dried sage, rosemary and basil.

monkey bread with apples & brown sugar
Prepare the basic recipe. In a plastic bag, shake 1 tablespoon ground cinnamon with 125g (4oz) brown sugar. Add 2 peeled and sliced apples, shake to coat, and layer in tin with dough balls.

bananas foster monkey bread
Prepare the basic recipe. In a plastic bag, shake 1 tablespoon cinnamon with 125g (4oz) brown sugar. Add 2 coarsely chopped bananas, shake to coat, and layer in tin with dough balls.

classic french baguette

see base recipe page 105

french baguette with chile & cheese
Prepare the basic recipe. Add 2 teaspoons crushed dried chilli flakes (or to taste) and 2 tablespoons finely grated Parmesan cheese to the flour before mixing. Just before baking, brush with a little melted butter and sprinkle with a little finely grated Parmesan cheese.

french baguette with garlic & thyme
Prepare the basic recipe. Add 2 garlic cloves, minced, and 2 teaspoons dried thyme to the flour before mixing. Brush with a little garlic oil just before baking.

french baguette with oregano & poppy seed
Prepare the basic recipe. Add 2 teaspoons dried oregano and 1 tablespoon poppy seeds to the flour before mixing.

french baguette with dill & sesame seed
Prepare the basic recipe. Add 2 teaspoons dried dill and 1 tablespoon sesame seeds to the flour before mixing. Brush with melted butter and a little dried dill just before baking.

pastries &
muffins

From time-consuming but impressive buttery

croissants to quick, fruity and savoury muffins, this

chapter has something for everyone.

fresh-from-the-oven pop tarts

see variations page 142

These are far superior to ready-made and quite simple to make. You can make them the day before and chill in fridge overnight.

225g (8z) flour
1 tbsp sugar
1 tsp salt
225g (8oz) unsalted butter, very cold and cubed
1 egg, beaten
2 tbsp cold milk (or less)

for the filling & glaze
125g (4oz) brown sugar
1½ tsp ground cinnamon
4 tsp flour
1 egg, beaten

In a large bowl, mix flour, sugar and salt. Using a pastry blender, cut in butter until it resembles coarse breadcrumbs. Add beaten egg and enough milk to just bring the dough together. Divide dough in half, wrap each piece in clingfilm and chill for 30 minutes. Remove dough from fridge and allow to soften a little, about 10 minutes. Remove clingfilm and roll each piece out on a lightly floured surface until each is a 25x30cm (10x12in) rectangle. Trim edges. Cut each piece into 8 smaller (8x13cm/3x5in) rectangles.

To make the filling, mix brown sugar, cinnamon and flour. Take 1 pastry rectangle, brush with beaten egg, then sprinkle a little of the filling in the middle, leaving a generous margin all around. Place another rectangle exactly on top and seal edges together with your fingers. Press with tines of a fork to seal completely, and then prick a few times to allow steam to escape during cooking. Repeat with the remaining pastry rectangles. Carefully place tarts on a greased, lined baking tray and brush with beaten egg to glaze. Refrigerate for 30 minutes (or overnight). Heat oven to 175˚C (350˚F/Gas mark 4) Remove tarts from fridge and bake for 25-35 minutes until light golden brown. Allow to cool before removing from baking tray.
Makes 8

cherry kuchen

see variations page 143

Kuchen is the German word for cake. This recipe is so quick to put together that you can have it on the table in 45 minutes.

225g (8oz) unsalted butter, softened
225g (8oz) sugar
2 large eggs
225g (8oz) flour
2 tsp baking powder

1 tsp vanilla extract
a little milk, if needed
1 x 450g (1lb) tin black cherry pie filling
40g (1½oz) flaked almonds
icing sugar, to dust

Preheat the oven to 175°C (350°F/Gas mark 4) and grease a 23x28cm (9x11in) baking tin. Mix the first six ingredients together to make a batter. If the batter is too thick, thin it with a little milk. Pour most of the batter into the bottom of the greased baking tin.

Pour the tin of black cherry pie filling on top and drop the remaining batter on top of the cherries. Scatter some flaked almonds on top. Bake for 35-40 minutes. Cool, then dust with icing sugar.

Serves 12

blueberry & white chocolate muffins

see variations page 144

The trick to making perfect muffins is to combine the wet ingredients from one bowl into the dry ingredients in another bowl as lightly and quickly as possible.

250g (9oz) flour
1 tbsp baking powder
pinch salt
125g (4oz) sugar
125g (4oz) white chocolate chips (or chopped white chocolate)

125g (4oz) fresh blueberries
2 large eggs
75g (3oz) unsalted butter, melted
250ml (9fl.oz) buttermilk
1 tsp vanilla extract

Preheat the oven to 200°C (400°F/Gas mark 6) and line a 12-cup muffin tin with paper muffin cups. In a bowl, sift together the flour, baking powder and salt. Stir in the sugar, white chocolate and blueberries. In another bowl, whisk the eggs, then whisk in the melted butter, buttermilk and vanilla extract.

Make a well in the centre of the dry ingredients and quickly pour in the wet ingredients. Stir quickly and lightly until just combined. It does not matter if there are a few lumps and dry bits. Spoon quickly into the muffin cups and bake for 20–25 minutes until golden, firm to the touch and well risen. Serve warm or cool on a wire rack.

Makes 12

danish pastries

see variations page 145

Baking with yeast can be very satisfying, especially when the end result is as delicious as these. You can start them the day before and let them rise in the refrigerator overnight.

4 tsp sugar
50ml (2fl.oz) lukewarm water
1 envelope active dried yeast
225g (8oz) plain flour
1 tsp salt
12g (½oz) white vegetable fat
1 large egg, lightly beaten

125g (4oz) unsalted butter
225g (8oz) almond paste
for the topping
1 egg, beaten
75g (3oz) icing sugar
1 tbsp milk

Dissolve 1 teaspoon sugar in warm water, then sprinkle yeast on top. Leave until frothy, 10–15 minutes. In a large bowl, mix flour with salt, then, using a pastry blender or your fingertips, cut in fat until mixture resembles fine breadcrumbs. Make a well in the centre and pour in yeast liquid, beaten egg and remaining sugar. Mix to a soft dough. Knead until dough is soft, smooth and elastic, using your fingers and knuckles. Alternatively, knead for 5 minutes in a mixer with a dough hook. Cover and leave in a cool place for 10 minutes.

Work the butter until it is a 23x8cm (9x3in) block. Roll out dough to a 25cm (10in) square and place butter block in the centre. Fold the dough sides up over it. Roll out dough to a 38x13cm (15x5in) oblong. Fold top third down and bottom third up. Put in a greased plastic bag and let rest for 20 minutes in the fridge. Repeat this process twice, finally resting for 40 minutes. At this stage you can rest the dough overnight in the fridge.

Roll out half the dough to a 25cm (10in) square, then cut it into four equal pieces. Fold two corners of each square to meet in the centre, like an envelope, and repeat with the other two corners. Press down firmly to seal. Place a small round of almond paste in the centre. Repeat with the remaining dough. Set pastries well apart on greased baking trays and cover loosely with clingfilm. Let rise in a warm place for 20 minutes.

Heat the oven to 220°C (425°F/Gas mark 7). Remove clingfilm and brush the pastries with lightly beaten egg. Bake for about 10 minutes, until golden brown. Mix the icing sugar and milk to make the glaze, and brush it over the pastries while they are still warm. Cool on a wire rack or serve warm.
Makes 8

crumble-topped cheese muffins

see variations page 146

Not everyone likes sweet muffins for breakfast. These savoury muffins have the benefit of protein as well.

250g (9oz) flour
1 tbsp baking powder
pinch salt
freshly ground black pepper
125g (4oz) grated Cheddar cheese
125g (4oz) chopped cooked ham
4 tbsp snipped fresh chives
2 large eggs
250ml (9fl.oz) buttermilk

75g (3oz) butter, melted
1 tsp French mustard

for the crumble topping
50g (2oz) flour
50g (2oz) cold butter
25g (1oz) grated Cheddar cheese
salt and freshly ground black pepper

Preheat the oven to 200°C (400°F/Gas mark 6) and line a 12-cup muffin tin with paper muffin cups. First make the crumble topping. Put the flour into a medium bowl and cut in the butter using a pastry blender or your fingertips until the mixture resembles fine breadcrumbs. Stir in the grated cheese and season with salt and pepper. Set aside.

In a large bowl, sift together the flour, baking powder, and salt and pepper to taste. Add the grated cheese, chopped ham and chives. In another bowl, whisk the eggs, then whisk in the buttermilk, melted butter and mustard. Make a well in the centre of the dry ingredients and quickly pour in the wet ingredients. Fold gently until just combined; do not overmix. Quickly spoon batter into the muffin cups and sprinkle with the crumble topping. Bake for about 20 minutes until golden brown, well risen, and firm to the touch. Serve warm, or cool on a wire rack.

Makes 12

jam doughnut muffins

see variations page 147

The sugar sprinkled on the muffins, and the jam inside, make these taste just like jam doughnuts.

250g (9oz) flour
1 tbsp baking powder
pinch salt
125g (4oz) granulated sugar
2 large eggs
175ml (6fl.oz) plus 2 tbsp milk
75g (3oz) butter, melted

1 tsp vanilla extract
4 tbsp good-quality strawberry jam

for the topping
50g (2oz) butter, melted
125g (4oz) sugar

Preheat the oven to 200°C (400°F/Gas mark 6) and line a 12-cup muffin tin with paper muffin cups. In a large bowl, sift the flour, baking powder and salt together. Add the sugar and stir to combine. In another bowl, whisk the eggs, then whisk in the milk, melted butter and vanilla extract. Make a well in the centre of the dry ingredients and quickly pour in the wet ingredients. Stir very gently until just combined; do not overmix. Spoon half the batter into the prepared muffin cups. Add a teaspoon of jam to the centre of each muffin, and then spoon in the rest of the batter. Bake for about 20 minutes until well risen, golden brown, and firm to the touch.

Prepare the topping while the muffins are cooking. Place the melted butter and sugar separately in two wide, shallow dishes. Cool the muffins for 5 minutes, then dip the top of each muffin in the melted butter and then dip in the sugar. Serve warm or cool on a wire rack.

Makes 12

pumpkin & pecan muffins

see variations page 148

These are moist and flavoured with autumn spices.

250g (9oz) flour
1 tbsp baking powder
½ tsp bicarbonate of soda
pinch salt
175g (6oz) brown sugar
75g (3oz) chopped pecans
1 tsp ground cinnamon
1 tsp pumpkin pie or mixed spice

2 large eggs
225ml (8fl.oz) soured cream
75g (3oz) butter, melted
1 tsp vanilla extract
175g (6oz) tinned pumpkin
12 pecan halves
3 tbsp maple syrup, to glaze

Preheat the oven to 200°C (400°F/Gas mark 6) and line a 12-cup muffin tin with paper muffin cups. In a large bowl, sift the flour, baking powder, bicarbonate of soda and salt together. Add the brown sugar, chopped pecans, cinnamon and mixed spice. Stir to combine. In another bowl, whisk the eggs, then whisk in the soured cream, melted butter, vanilla extract and pumpkin.

Make a well in the centre of the dry ingredients and quickly pour in the wet ingredients, stirring quickly and gently until just combined. Spoon into the muffin cups and top each muffin with a pecan half. Bake for about 20 minutes until golden brown, well risen and firm to the touch.

Cool the muffins in the tin for 5 minutes, then brush them with the maple syrup to glaze. Serve warm, or cool on a wire rack.
Makes 12

wholemeal muesli &
sunflower seed muffins

see variations page 149

The sunflower seeds add a wonderful crunch to these muffins, and the sunflower oil is healthier than butter.

125g (4oz) plain flour
50g (2oz) wholemeal flour
1 tbsp baking powder
pinch salt
25g (1oz) rolled oats
2 tbsp wheat bran
125g (4oz) raisins

175g (6oz) brown sugar
50g (2oz) sunflower seeds
2 large eggs
250ml (9fl.oz) buttermilk
6 tbsp sunflower oil (or substitute
    vegetable oil)
1 tsp vanilla extract

Preheat the oven to 200°C (400°F/Gas mark 6) and line a 12-cup muffin tin with paper muffin cups. In a large bowl, sift together the flours, baking powder and salt. Stir in the rolled oats, wheat bran, raisins, brown sugar and sunflower seeds. In another bowl, whisk the eggs, then whisk in the buttermilk, sunflower oil and vanilla extract.

Make a well in the centre of the dry ingredients and quickly pour in the wet ingredients. Stir gently until just combined; do not overmix. Spoon batter into the muffin cups and bake for about 20 minutes until well risen, golden brown and firm to the touch. Serve warm, or cool on a wire rack.

Makes 12

banana, cranberry & walnut muffins

see variations page 150

Bananas make a wonderful addition to muffins because they add a delicious moistness.

225g (8oz) plain flour
25g (1oz) wholemeal flour
1 tbsp. baking powder
½ tsp salt
2 tbsp rolled oats
175g (6oz) brown sugar
75g (3oz) chopped walnuts
50g (2oz) dried cranberries
2 large bananas

2 large eggs, lightly beaten
225ml (8fl.oz) buttermilk
6 tbsp sunflower or vegetable oil
1 tsp vanilla extract

for topping
3 tbsp apricot jam
50g (2oz) chopped walnuts

Preheat the oven to 200°C (400°F/Gas mark 6) and line a 12-cup muffin tin with paper muffin cups. In a large bowl, sift together the flours, baking powder and salt. Stir in the rolled oats, brown sugar, walnuts and cranberries. In another bowl, mash the bananas, then stir in the beaten eggs, buttermilk, oil and vanilla extract.

Make a well in the centre of the dry ingredients and quickly pour in the wet ingredients, stirring gently until just combined. Do not overmix. Spoon into the muffin cups and bake for about 20 minutes until well risen, golden brown and firm to the touch. Leave to cool in the tin for 5 minutes. Gently heat the jam and brush it on top of the muffins, then sprinkle with the walnuts. Serve warm, or cool on a wire rack.

Makes 12

heart-friendly muffins

see variations page 151

Though low in saturated fat, these are absolutely delicious. They're best eaten within a day of baking.

200g (7oz) plain flour
25g (1oz) wholemeal flour
1 tbsp baking powder
zest of 1 lemon
125g (4oz) granulated sugar
50g (2oz) brown sugar
1 banana
1 egg, beaten

300ml (10fl.oz) buttermilk
5 tbsp vegetable oil
125g (4oz) blueberries

for glaze
2 tsp freshly squeezed lemon juice
1 tbsp granulated sugar

Preheat the oven to 200°C (400°F/Gas mark 6) and line a 12-cup muffin tin with paper muffin cups. In a large bowl, sift together the flours and baking powder. Stir in the lemon zest and the sugars. In another bowl, mash the banana, then stir in the beaten egg, buttermilk and oil.

Make a well in the centre of the dry ingredients, then quickly pour in the wet ingredients, stirring gently until just combined. Do not overmix. Add the blueberries and give just a few turns to combine them without crushing them. Spoon the mixture into the muffin cups and bake for about 20 minutes until well risen, golden brown and firm to the touch. While the muffins are cooling for 5 minutes, mix the sugar and lemon juice together and brush over the muffins to glaze them while they are still hot. Serve warm, or cool on a wire rack.

Makes 12

parmesan & pine nut muffins

see variations page 152

With their hint of garlic, these savoury muffins will fill your kitchen with a wonderful aroma.

250g (9oz) flour
1 tbsp baking powder
pinch salt
freshly ground black pepper to taste
25g (1oz) finely grated Parmesan cheese
50g (2oz) pine nuts
1 tsp garlic powder
1 tbsp dried Italian herbs

2 large eggs
1 tsp French mustard
250ml (9fl.oz) buttermilk
6 tbsp. sunflower oil

for topping
2 tbsp finely grated Parmesan cheese
2 tbsp pine nuts

Preheat the oven to 200°C (400°F/Gas mark 6) and line a 12-cup muffin tin with paper muffin cups. In a large bowl, sift together the flour, baking powder and salt. Add the black pepper, Parmesan cheese, pine nuts, garlic powder and herbs. Stir until combined. In another bowl, whisk the eggs, then whisk in the mustard, buttermilk and sunflower oil.

Make a well in the centre of the dry ingredients, then quickly pour in the wet ingredients, stirring gently until just combined. Do not overmix. Spoon batter into the muffin cups, then sprinkle on the Parmesan cheese and pine nuts for the topping. Bake for about 20 minutes until well risen, golden brown and firm to the touch. Cool in the tin for 5 minutes, then serve warm.

Makes 12

flaky croissants

see variations page 153

Although a simplified version, these are still quite time-consuming, so start them the day before and refrigerate overnight. In the morning, bring them back to room temperature and let rise until doubled in size, an hour or so, before baking. These also freeze well. Freeze, uncovered, immediately upon forming into crescents. Cover once frozen. Defrost overnight, then let rise until doubled.

225ml (8fl.oz) warm milk
50g (2oz) plus 1 tsp sugar
1 envelope active dried yeast
125g (4oz) plain or white bread flour
1 egg, beaten
125g (4oz) butter, softened, not melted

450g (1lb) white bread flour
1 tsp salt
225g (8oz) butter, very cold
1 tsp sugar
2 tsp water
1 egg, beaten

Stir the warm milk and 1 teaspoon sugar together. Add yeast, then set aside until frothy, about 10 minutes. Add flour and beat well. Add remaining sugar and egg, and beat again until smooth. Add butter, beat, and set aside. Put the 450g (1lb) flour and salt into the bowl of a food processor. Add the 225g (8oz) butter, cut into small cubes, and pulse briefly until butter is the size of peas. The idea now is to get a soft dough without melting the pieces of butter, so it needs to stay really cold. Tip flour and butter mixture into a large bowl, add milk and yeast mixture and mix until moistened. Cover bowl and refrigerate for 2 hours.

Remove from fridge, turn out onto a lightly floured surface, and knead lightly, then roll dough into a rectangle about 45x30cm (18x12in) in size. Working as quickly as possible, fold the dough into thirds, bringing the bottom third up and folding the top third over. Put into a

greased plastic bag and back in the fridge for 1 hour. Repeat the rolling and chilling twice more. You can leave dough in the fridge overnight at this stage. Divide dough into four parts. Keep three parts chilled, and roll out the fourth into a circle about 30cm (12in) across. Cut circle into six pie-shaped wedges. For each croissant, with your fingers roll each wedge from the wide edge towards the point, stretching the dough slightly as you roll. Curl them into crescents, place on floured baking trays, and cover loosely. Repeat with remaining dough. Let crescents rise at room temperature until doubled in size. This could take 2 hours. Preheat oven to 200°C (400°F/Gas mark 6). Make egg wash by mixing the sugar and water, then adding the egg. Remove cover from croissants, brush with egg wash, and put into the oven. Immediately turn temperature down to 175°C (350°F/Gas mark 4) and bake for 15-20 minutes until golden.

Makes 24

variations

fresh-from-the-oven pop tarts

see base recipe page 119

berry pop tarts
Prepare the basic recipe. Replace the filling and beaten egg with 2 teaspoons good-quality berry jam (strawberry or raspberry both work well) per tart. After baking, glaze with a little icing sugar mixed with a little water.

chocolate chip pop tarts
Prepare the basic recipe. Replace the filling and beaten egg with 2 teaspoons chocolate chips per tart. After baking, glaze with a little icing sugar mixed with a little water.

apple strudel pop tarts
Prepare the basic recipe. Replace the filling with a mixture of 2 teaspoons tinned apple pie filling and a few sultanas and a little ground cinnamon to spread on each tart.

apricot & almond pop tarts
Prepare the basic recipe, omitting the filling and beaten egg. Substitute 2 teaspoons good-quality apricot jam for each one. Sprinkle with some flaked almonds. After baking, glaze with a little icing sugar mixed with a little water.

variations

cherry kuchen

see base recipe page 120

apricot & almond kuchen
Prepare the basic recipe, adding 1 teaspoon almond extract to the batter.
Instead of the cherry filling, drain 1 (450g/1lb) tin apricots. Heat juice with
2 tablespoons cornflour and 2 tablespoons orange juice until boiling and
thickened. Chop apricots, add to the juice and cool before using.

apple & cinnamon kuchen
Prepare the basic recipe, replacing the butter with 225ml (8fl.oz) vegetable oil.
Instead of the cherry filling, stew 2 peeled and sliced apples with 2 tablespoons
sugar and 2 teaspoons cinnamon. Cool before using.

plum kuchen
Prepare the basic recipe, omitting the cherries. Substitute 450g (1lb) pitted and
chopped plums, stewed gently in a little water and a little sugar to taste. Cool
before using.

rhubarb & orange kuchen
Prepare the basic recipe, omitting the cherries. Substitute 450g (1lb) sliced
rhubarb, stewed in a little orange juice and sugar to taste. Thicken with
cornflour if needed. Cool before using.

variations

blueberry & white chocolate muffins

see base recipe page 123

cherry, coconut & white chocolate muffins

Prepare the basic recipe, omitting the blueberries and 25g (1oz) of white
chocolate chips. Add 25g (1oz) unsweetened desiccated coconut and 225g (8oz)
pitted and chopped fresh cherries.

blueberry & chocolate muffins

Prepare the basic recipe, replacing the white chocolate chips with plain
chocolate chips.

raspberry & white chocolate muffins

Prepare the basic recipe, replacing the blueberries with 125g (4oz)
fresh raspberries.

double chocolate blueberry muffins

Prepare the basic recipe, replacing 25g (1oz) white chocolate chips with
25g (1oz) plain chocolate chips.

blueberry fruit explosion muffins

Prepare the basic recipe, replacing the white chocolate chips with 25g (1oz)
each dried cherries, cranberries, raisins and chopped dried dates.

variations

danish pastries

see base recipe page 124

pecan pinwheels
Prepare basic recipe. Cut each pastry square almost to the middle from each corner. Make a filling with 75g (3oz) ground pecans, 1 tablespoon maple syrup, and 50g (2oz) brown sugar. Place 1 teaspoon filling in middle of each square and fold in each point of pastry. Continue with the basic recipe, adding some chopped pecans mixed with a little sugar on top of the egg wash before baking.

danish pastries with apricot
Prepare basic recipe. Place 2 teaspoons custard in middle of each square. Top with 2 tinned apricot halves and dot with apricot jam. Fold 2 corners into middle and pinch to seal. Continue with basic recipe.

danish pastries with strawberry
Prepare basic recipe. Place 2 teaspoons custard in middle of each square. Top with strawberries and dot with strawberry jam. Fold 2 corners into middle and pinch to seal. Continue with basic recipe.

raisin whirls
Prepare basic recipe, but roll pastry into a rectangle. Make a filling with 50g (2oz) raisins, 50g (2oz) sugar, 50g (2oz) soft butter, and 1 teaspoon pumpkin pie or mixed spice. Spread over dough, roll up like a swiss roll, cut into slices and press each one down on baking tray. Continue with basic recipe.

crumble-topped ham & cheese muffins

see base recipe page 126

crumble-topped rosemary, ham & cheese muffins
Prepare the basic recipe, omitting the chopped chives and substituting
4 teaspoons chopped dried rosemary.

crumble-topped sausage & cheese muffins
Prepare the basic recipe, replacing the ham and chives with 125g (4oz)
chopped, cooked, spicy sausage and 2 tablespoons dried sage.

crumble-topped courgette & cheese muffins
Prepare the basic recipe, replacing the ham and chives with 125g (4oz)
chopped, cooked courgettes and 2 tablespoons dried oregano.

crumble-topped spinach & nutmeg muffins
Prepare the basic recipe, replacing the ham and chives with 125g (4oz)
chopped, cooked spinach and 2 teaspoons ground nutmeg.

crumble-topped carrot & coriander muffins
Prepare the basic recipe, replacing the ham and chives with 125g (4oz)
grated peeled carrots and 2 tablespoons freshly chopped coriander.

variations

jam doughnut muffins

see base recipe page 129

raspberry & coconut doughnut muffins
Prepare the basic recipe, adding 25g (1oz) unsweetened desiccated coconut to
the batter. Replace the strawberry jam with raspberry jam.

apricot & almond doughnut muffins
Prepare the basic recipe, replacing the vanilla extract with almond extract and
the strawberry jam with apricot jam.

black cherry doughnut muffins
Prepare the basic recipe, replacing the strawberry jam with black cherry jam.

lemon & black currant doughnut muffins
Prepare the basic recipe, adding 2 teaspoons finely grated lemon zest to the
muffin batter. Replace the strawberry jam with blackcurrant jam.

orange doughnut muffins
Prepare the basic recipe, replacing the strawberry jam with orange marmalade.

variations

pumpkin & pecan muffins

see base recipe page 130

butternut squash & walnut muffins
Prepare the basic recipe, replacing the tinned pumpkin with 175g (6oz) cooked butternut squash pulp and the pecans with 75g (3oz) chopped walnuts. Top the muffins with walnut halves.

carrot & coriander muffins
Prepare the basic recipe, replacing the tinned pumpkin with 175g (6oz) cooked and mashed carrots and the mixed spice with 2 tablespoons chopped fresh coriander.

courgette & chocolate chip muffins
Prepare the basic recipe, replacing the tinned pumpkin with 175g (6oz) cooked, chopped courgettes and the pecans with 50g (2oz) plain chocolate chips.

pumpkin, pecan & raisin muffins
Prepare the basic recipe, adding 150g (5oz) raisins to the batter.

pumpkin, fig & pistachio muffins
Prepare the basic recipe, replacing the pecans with 125g (4oz) chopped dried figs and 25g (1oz) shelled chopped pistachios.

variations

wholemeal muesli & sunflower seed muffins

see base recipe page 133

wholemeal ginger & apple spice muffins
Prepare the basic recipe, omitting half the raisins and adding 50g (2oz)
chopped apple, 3 teaspoons ground ginger, 2 teaspoons ground cinnamon
and 2 teaspoons ground nutmeg.

wholemeal maple oatmeal muffins
Prepare the basic recipe, replacing 125ml (4fl.oz) of the buttermilk with
125ml (4fl.oz) maple syrup.

wholemeal peach muesli muffins
Prepare the basic recipe, replacing half the raisins with 125g (4oz) chopped
fresh or tinned peaches.

wholemeal fruit & courgette bran muffins
Prepare the basic recipe, replacing half the raisins with 125g (4oz) cooked
and chopped courgettes.

wholemeal trail mix muffins
Prepare the basic recipe, replacing the rolled oats with a ready-made
trail mix.

variations

banana, cranberry & walnut muffins

see base recipe page 134

banana, peach & almond muffins
Prepare the basic recipe, replacing the vanilla extract with almond extract, the walnuts with almonds, and the cranberries with 125g (4oz) chopped tinned or fresh peaches.

banana, apple & cinnamon muffins
Prepare the basic recipe, replacing the cranberries with 125g (4oz) peeled, cored and chopped apples. Add 2 teaspoons ground cinnamon to the dry ingredients.

banana, mocha & pecan muffins
Prepare the basic recipe, replacing the cranberries and walnuts with 50g (2oz) plain chocolate chips and 75g (3oz) chopped pecans. Add 3 teaspoons instant coffee granules to the dry ingredients.

whole wheat banana, cranberry & walnut muffins
Prepare the basic recipe, replacing 125g (4oz) of the plain flour with 125g (4oz) wholemeal flour.

variations

heart-friendly muffins

see base recipe page 137

heart-friendly fig & bran muffins
Prepare the basic recipe, replacing the blueberries with 125g (4oz) chopped dried figs and replacing 25g (1oz) flour with 25g (1oz) wheat bran.

heart-friendly date & walnut muffins
Prepare the basic recipe, omitting 50g (2oz) blueberries and adding 25g (1oz) chopped dates, 25g (1oz) raisins, and 50g (2oz) chopped walnuts.

heart-friendly sultanas & bran muffins
Prepare the basic recipe, replacing 50g (2oz) blueberries with 50g (2oz) sultanas and 25g (1oz) plain flour with 25g (1oz) wheat bran.

heart-friendly spicy apple & oatmeal muffins
Prepare the basic recipe, replacing the blueberries with 175g (6oz) peeled, cored, and chopped apples and 50g (2oz) of the plain flour with 50g (2oz) rolled oats. Add 2 teaspoons mixed spice to the dry ingredients.

heart-friendly muffins with ginger
Prepare the basic recipe, adding 25g (1oz) chopped crystallised ginger to the dry ingredients.

parmesan & pine nut muffins

see base recipe page 138

tuna & olive muffins
Prepare the basic recipe, omitting the cheese, pine nuts, and mustard.
Substitute 50g (2oz) pitted, chopped black olives and 1 (175g/6oz) tin
of tuna in oil, drained and flaked. Omit the topping.

chicken & corn muffins
Prepare the basic recipe, omitting the Parmesan, pine nuts, and mustard.
Substitute 50g (2oz) tinned sweetcorn and 125g (4oz) chopped cooked
chicken breast. Replace the topping with a sprinkling of paprika.

spicy sausage & onion muffins
Prepare the basic recipe, replacing the Parmesan and pine nuts with
50g (2oz) cooked and chopped spicy sausage and 50g (2oz) cooked
chopped onion. Omit the topping.

spinach, parmesan & pine nut muffins
Prepare the basic recipe, adding 50g (2oz) cooked, chopped and drained spinach.

crispy bacon & cheese muffins
Prepare the basic recipe, replacing the Parmesan and pine nuts with 25g (1oz)
grated Cheddar cheese and 50g (2oz) crisply cooked and crumbled bacon.

variations

flaky croissants

see base recipe page 140

chocolate-filled croissants
Prepare the basic recipe, but just before rolling up the dough, place a small square of chocolate at the wide edge of the triangle.

almond croissants
Prepare the basic recipe, but just before rolling up the dough, place a small ball of almond paste at the wide edge of the triangle. Scatter a few flaked almonds over the tops of all the croissants before baking.

croissants with raisins
Prepare the basic recipe, but just before rolling up the dough, sprinkle a teaspoon of raisins over the dough and press them in slightly.

ham & cheese breakfast croissant sandwich
Prepare the basic recipe. Slice croissants in half, add 2 slices of ham and 1 slice mild processed cheese per croissant, and warm in oven to melt the cheese.

snack-size croissants
Prepare the basic recipe. Instead of dividing the dough into 4 parts, divide into 8 parts. Roll into circles 15cm (6in) across, then follow the basic recipe.

eggs

Eggs are pure protein and very versatile. Low in calories and carbohydrates, they are the ideal food to sustain you until lunchtime. They are quick and easy to cook, go with anything and you'll never get tired of them.

perfect poached eggs

see variations page 172

If you know how to make poached eggs perfectly, then you can make lots of perfect egg dishes for any number of people. Make sure you have everything to hand before you start to cook, as these eggs take very little time to prepare.

2 eggs
1 tsp white vinegar
hot buttered toast, to serve

Crack the eggs into small ramekins and set aside. Fill a medium saucepan two-thirds full with water, add white vinegar and bring to the boil. Turn the heat down and get the water to a rolling boil, that is, just past the simmering point, but not so that the bubbles are moving really strongly. If the water is boiling too much, it will disperse the egg as you tip it in.

When you are happy with the water, tip your egg into the middle. The water swirling around the edge will help keep the egg together. Time the egg for 2½ minutes (for a large egg). It will start to rise to the surface as it cooks. Lift out carefully with a slotted spoon and drain on kitchen towel. Repeat with the other egg. Serve on hot buttered toast.

Serves 2

soft-boiled eggs & soldiers

see variations page 173

This is a favourite British breakfast dish. The eggs are served in egg cups, and the toast strips, known as 'soldiers', are dipped into the runny egg yolk. Always buy the same size eggs and you will get to know the exact timing for how thick or runny you like your soft-boiled egg to be.

2 eggs
2-4 slices thick white bread
butter, for spreading

Place your eggs in a saucepan of cold water and put the pan on a burner. Turn the heat to the highest setting and bring the water to the boil, uncovered. As soon as the water starts to boil, lower the heat and simmer for between 3 and 5 minutes, depending on the size of the egg. Practice and experience are important.

Meanwhile, toast the bread slices on both sides under the grill or in a toaster, spread them with butter and cut them into strips.

Remove the eggs from the pan with a slotted spoon, place in egg cups, and surround with the toast strips. Serve immediately.

Serves 2

ham & cheese soufflé

see variations page 174

Soufflés need to be served as soon as they come out of the oven, as they can deflate quite quickly.

50g (2oz) butter, plus extra for greasing
50g (2oz) flour
175ml (6fl.oz) whole milk
3 large eggs, separated
175g (6oz) finely chopped ham

1 tsp Dijon-style mustard
125g (4oz) grated Cheddar cheese, plus 1 tbsp
    for sprinkling
salt and freshly ground black pepper

Heat the oven to 190°C (375°F/Gas mark 5) and liberally butter a 1-litre (2-pint) soufflé dish (or four ramekin dishes) Melt butter in a large saucepan, add the flour and cook for a minute, stirring constantly. Remove from the heat and gradually stir in the milk. Return to the heat and bring to the boil, stirring all the time, until it becomes a thick sauce that leaves the sides of the pan. Stir in the egg yolks, ham, mustard and the cheese. Season with salt and freshly ground black pepper. Keep over the heat, stirring all the time, until the cheese has melted. Remove from the heat.

In a clean bowl, whisk the egg whites until stiff peaks form. Fold whites into the cheese sauce with a metal spoon. Turn mixture into the buttered soufflé dish (or four buttered ramekin dishes) and run a teaspoon around the outside edge of the mixture, pushing it inward to prevent the soufflé spilling over when cooking. Sprinkle 1 tablespoon grated Cheddar over the top, and bake for 40 minutes until well risen and golden brown. Remove from oven and serve immediately.

Serves 4

full english frittata

see variations page 175

A frittata (an Italian word for an omelette) is baked in the oven. This one has all the elements of a full English breakfast in it.

1 tbsp olive oil, plus extra for greasing
8 large eggs
50ml (2fl.oz) soured cream
salt and freshly ground black pepper
5 rashers bacon, chopped into bite-size pieces

125g (4oz) sliced button mushrooms
5 cooked chipolatas, cut into bite-size pieces
4 cooked, peeled potatoes, cut into bite-size pieces
1 tbsp freshly chopped parsley

Heat the oven to 175°C (350°F/Gas mark 4) and grease a 23x32.5cm (9x13in) rectangular baking dish with olive oil. In a large bowl, whisk the eggs, then whisk in the soured cream and salt and pepper to taste. Set aside.

In a large frying pan, heat 1 tablespoon oil, and fry the bacon and mushrooms until nicely browned and slightly caramelized. Add the chipolatas, potato pieces and parsley, and heat through.

Tip the contents of the pan into the baking dish, then pour in the egg mixture. Bake for about 35 minutes, or until the egg has risen and set. Serve immediately.

Serves 4

ultimate spanish tortilla

see variations page 176

A Spanish tortilla is a thick omelette made with potatoes and onions.

6 or 7 potatoes, peeled
4 tbsp olive oil
1 small onion, finely chopped

salt and freshly ground black pepper
8 large eggs

In a large saucepan, boil the potatoes for 10 minutes. Drain, leave to cool, then thinly slice. In a frying pan, heat the oil, then fry the onion until softened. Add the sliced potatoes and fry until lightly browned, not crisp. Season with salt and freshly ground black pepper.

In a bowl, whisk the eggs, then pour them into the frying pan on top of the potatoes and onions. Cook over medium heat until the eggs have just set and the bottom has browned. Turn the tortilla out onto a plate, then slide it back into the pan to cook the other side. (Alternatively, after cooking the first side, heat the grill and grill the top of the tortilla until browned.) Serve immediately, cut into wedges.

Serves 4

mexican scrambled eggs

see variations page 177

Scrambled eggs are a good foundation for a multitude of flavourful ingredients. This Mexican recipe, with its tortilla strips, tomatoes and pepper, can be easily varied.

3 tbsp vegetable oil
3 soft tortillas
2 fresh tomatoes, deseeded and chopped
3 spring onions, chopped
1 green jalapeño pepper, deseeded and chopped

8 eggs, beaten
salt and freshly ground black pepper
2 tbsp. freshly chopped coriander, to garnish

In a large frying pan, heat the vegetable oil. Roll up the tortillas and slice them into strips directly into the hot oil. Fry them for a few minutes until crisp, then remove them from the pan and drain on a paper towel.

Add the chopped tomatoes, spring onions and jalapeño to the frying pan, and fry together for 2 minutes. Tip the tortillas back into the pan and add the beaten eggs. Season to taste with salt and pepper. Stir with a wooden spoon to scramble the eggs. Once the eggs start to set, remove the frying pan from the heat and continue to stir until cooked to your liking. Serve immediately, sprinkled with chopped coriander.

Serves 4

crabmeat strata

see variations page 178

This is a very rich and creamy dish, especially good for a holiday brunch buffet. It can be prepared up to 24 hours in advance.

butter, for greasing
6 thick slices white bread, cut into cubes
2 (175g/6oz) tins crabmeat or 450g (1lb) fresh
   crabmeat, picked over
125g (4oz) grated Gruyère cheese
125g (4oz) grated Cheddar cheese

4 spring onions, roughly chopped
6 large eggs, lightly beaten
300ml (10fl.oz) milk
2 tbsp dry sherry or apple juice
1 tbsp Dijon mustard
1 tbsp Worcestershire sauce

Grease a 1-litre (2-pint) casserole dish with butter. In a large bowl, mix together the bread, crabmeat, cheeses and spring onions. Add the remaining ingredients and stir well to combine. Pour into the casserole, cover and chill for 2–24 hours.

Heat the oven to 175°C (350°F/Gas mark 4). Remove the cover from the casserole and bake for about 45 minutes, or until a knife inserted in the middle comes out clean. Leave to stand for 10 minutes before serving.

Serves 6-8

squash, sage & gruyère frittata

see variations page 179

These are some interesting flavours for breakfast, if you fancy something different.

25g (1oz) butter
450lb (1lb) butternut squash in 5mm (¼in)
   cubes (about 2 medium squash)
2 tbsp freshly chopped sage

8 large eggs
50ml (2fl.oz) water
75g (3oz) grated Gruyère cheese
salt and freshly ground black pepper

In a large ovenproof frying pan, melt the butter, add the squash and sauté for about 8-10 minutes. Stir in the sage. Cook until the squash is tender and slightly browned.

Heat the grill. In a large bowl, whisk the eggs and water together and stir in half the cheese. Season with salt and pepper and pour over the squash in the frying pan. Reduce the heat, cover and cook for a few minutes until the eggs are beginning to set on the bottom but the top is still a little loose. Remove the cover, sprinkle the remaining cheese on top, and place frying pan under the grill. Grill until just set and the cheese is melted. Leave to stand for 10 minutes, then serve, cut into wedges.

Serves 4-5

eggs florentine

see variations page 180

Once you've perfected your poached egg technique, there are many ways to turn them into a delicious, filling breakfast, such as this one with spinach, hollandaise sauce and muffins.

2 egg yolks
2 tbsp. hot water
175g (6oz) butter, melted
juice of ½ lemon
salt and freshly ground black pepper

pinch cayenne pepper
50g (2oz) butter for cooking and spreading
350g (12oz) fresh spinach leaves
4 poached eggs (page 155)
2 muffins, split

First make a hollandaise sauce. Place the egg yolks in a heat-resistant glass bowl over a pan of simmering water and whisk with 2 tablespoons hot water. Very slowly, add the melted butter. Do not add the milky residue at the bottom of the melted butter. Whisk until all the butter has been incorporated. Whisk in the lemon juice and season with salt and a pinch of cayenne pepper. Set aside.

In a large frying pan, melt a little butter and add the spinach. Stir until wilted, then drain and season with salt and pepper. Remove from heat. Heat the grill and toast the muffins until lightly browned. Spread with butter and divide the spinach between them, leaving a slight indentation on top in which to place the poached eggs, one on each muffin half. Spoon a quarter of the hollandaise over each egg, then place them underneath the grill for 1 minute. Serve immediately.

Serves 2-4

bacon & egg tarts

see variations page 181

Make these tarts when you want to impress your guests.

12g (½oz) butter for greasing
275g (10oz) shortcrust pastry (homemade or
    ready-made)
8 rashers bacon, chopped
1 small onion, finely chopped

2 large eggs
175ml (6fl.oz) whipping cream
salt and freshly ground black pepper
2 tbsp freshly chopped parsley

Preheat the oven to 200°C (400°F/Gas mark 6), and grease 4 individual 10cm (4in) tart tins
with butter.

On a lightly floured surface, roll out the pastry, then line the 4 tart tins. Line pastry with
waxed paper, fill with baking beans, and bake for 10 minutes. Remove the paper and beans
and bake for 5 more minutes. Remove tins from the oven.

In a frying pan, fry the bacon for a few minutes, add the onion and continue to cook until
the onion has softened and the bacon is crisp. Divide the bacon and onion between the tart
tins. In a bowl, whisk the eggs and cream together, and season with salt and pepper. Stir in
the parsley. Divide mixture between the tart tins.

Place the tart tins on a baking tray (which makes it easier to move them in and out of the
oven). Bake for about 15-20 minutes, until the eggs have set and the tarts are golden brown.
Serve immediately.

Serves 4

variations

perfect poached eggs

see base recipe page 155

poached eggs on crushed potatoes
Prepare the basic recipe, but instead of serving the eggs on hot buttered toast, serve on boiled potatoes, crushed with a little butter and parsley.

poached eggs with asparagus
Prepare the basic recipe, but instead of serving the eggs on hot buttered toast, serve with some steamed asparagus, dressed with melted butter and parsley.

poached eggs with bagels
Prepare the basic recipe, but instead of serving the eggs on hot buttered toast, serve them on halved bagels, spread with a little cream cheese or butter.

poached eggs with mushrooms & ham
Prepare the basic recipe, but instead of serving the eggs on hot buttered toast, serve them on portobello mushrooms.

soft-boiled eggs & soldiers

see base recipe page 156

hard-boiled eggs with bagel soldiers
Prepare the basic recipe, boiling the eggs for an extra 7 or 8 minutes. Remove from heat and put the eggs into iced water for 5 minutes. Remove shells, mash eggs with a little mayonnaise, add salt and pepper to taste, and spread on bagels cut into soldiers.

soft-boiled eggs with sausage dippers
Prepare the basic recipe, replacing the bread and butter with cooked chipolatas to dip in the egg.

soft-boiled eggs with asparagus
Prepare the basic recipe, replacing the bread and butter with steamed asparagus to dip in the egg.

soft-boiled eggs with thick oven fries
Prepare the basic recipe, replacing the bread and butter with thick oven fries. Peel and slice a large potato into thick strips, coat with vegetable oil, and bake at 200°C (400°F/Gas mark 6) for 30 minutes. Serve hot with the eggs.

variations

ham & cheese soufflé

see base recipe page 159

mushroom & cheese soufflé
Prepare the basic recipe, replacing the ham with 125g (4oz) cooked, sliced button mushrooms.

ham, cheese & onion soufflé
Prepare the basic recipe, adding 1 finely chopped onion. Sauté for a few minutes in the melted butter before adding the flour.

ham & double cheese soufflé
Prepare the basic recipe, replacing half the Cheddar cheese with mozzarella cheese.

ham, cheese & spinach soufflé
Prepare the basic recipe, adding 175g (6oz) cooked, well-drained, chopped spinach to the mixture.

tuna & cheese soufflé
Prepare the basic recipe, replacing the ham with tinned tuna, drained and flaked.

full english frittata

see base recipe page 160

potato, apple & tuna frittata
Prepare the basic recipe, omitting the bacon and sausage and adding 1 peeled, cored and chopped apple and 1 tin (175g/6oz) tuna, drained and flaked, before mixing with the eggs.

smoked salmon frittata
Prepare the basic recipe, omitting the bacon and sausage. Add 175g (6oz) chopped smoked salmon before mixing with the eggs.

cheese & onion frittata
Prepare the basic recipe, omitting the sausage. Add 1 finely chopped onion and cook it with the bacon. Stir 125g (4oz) grated Cheddar cheese into the eggs.

feta & pepper frittata
Prepare the basic recipe, omitting the bacon and sausage, and adding 1 deseeded and sliced red pepper to the mixture with the mushrooms, and 125g (4oz) chopped feta with the parsley.

variations

ultimate spanish tortilla

see base recipe page 162

spanish tortilla with cheese & leeks
Prepare the basic recipe, adding 1 chopped leek to the frying pan with the
onion, and 75g (3oz) grated Cheddar cheese to the frying pan with the eggs.

spanish tortilla with parma ham & basil
Prepare the basic recipe, adding 125g (4oz) chopped Parma ham and
3 tablespoons freshly grated basil to the frying pan with the eggs.

spanish tortilla with chorizo & parsley
Prepare the basic recipe, adding 125g (4oz) chopped chorizo and
3 tablespoons freshly chopped parsley to the frying pan with the eggs.

spanish tortilla with spring onion & peas
Prepare the basic recipe, adding 3 chopped spring onions and 50g (2oz)
frozen peas to the frying pan with the eggs.

mexican scrambled eggs

see base recipe page 163

mexican scrambled eggs with vegetables
Prepare the basic recipe, adding 25g (1oz) each of finely chopped red pepper, mushrooms and Spanish onion to the frying pan with the tomatoes.

spanish scrambled eggs
Prepare the basic recipe, omitting the jalapeño pepper and substituting 50g (2oz) spicy chorizo sausage, chopped into tiny cubes.

french scrambled eggs
Prepare the basic recipe, omitting the tortilla, jalapeño pepper and coriander. Substitute 50g (2oz) cooked potato, cut into tiny cubes, 1 crushed garlic clove and parsley.

swiss scrambled eggs
Prepare the basic recipe, omitting the jalapeño pepper and substituting cooked and finely grated potato to the eggs.

variations

crabmeat strata

see base recipe page 164

smoked salmon strata
Prepare the basic recipe, replacing the crabmeat with tinned red salmon, drained and flaked.

shrimp, egg & parsley strata
Prepare the basic recipe, replacing the crabmeat with 125g (4oz) cooked small prawns, 2 chopped hard-boiled eggs and 2 tablespoons freshly chopped parsley.

crab & tuna strata
Prepare the basic recipe, replacing 1 tin crabmeat with 1 tin tuna, drained and flaked.

mushroom, leek & cheese strata
Prepare the basic recipe, omitting the crabmeat and substituting 125g (4oz) cooked and sliced mushrooms and 125g (4oz) cooked and chopped leeks.

smoked mackerel & tomato strata
Prepare the basic recipe, replacing the crabmeat with smoked mackerel, bones removed and chopped. Add 2 tomatoes, deseeded and chopped.

variations

squash, sage & gruyère frittata

see base recipe page 166

courgette, thyme & gruyère frittata
Prepare the basic recipe, replacing the butternut squash with courgettes and the sage with fresh thyme leaves.

carrot, coriander & gruyère frittata
Prepare the basic recipe, replacing the squash with 450g (1lb) boiled and chopped carrots and the sage with fresh coriander.

broccoli, oregano & gruyère frittata
Prepare the basic recipe, replacing the squash with 450g (1lb) cooked and chopped broccoli and the sage with fresh oregano.

squash, scallion, pancetta & gruyère frittata
Prepare the basic recipe, adding 4 chopped spring onions and 125g (4oz) chopped pancetta to the frying pan with the sage.

variations

eggs florentine

see base recipe page 169

eggs benedict
Prepare the basic recipe, replacing the spinach with a slice of bacon or ham, lightly sautéed in a little butter, on each muffin.

sausage & tomato eggs benedict
Prepare the basic recipe, replacing the spinach with a cooked sausage patty (homemade if desired; see recipe page 233) topped with a slice of tomato, sautéed lightly in butter.

eggs florentine with cheese
Prepare the basic recipe, adding a slice of cheese on top of the muffin before you add the poached egg.

eggs florentine with mustard hollandaise
Prepare the basic recipe, adding 1 teaspoon Dijon mustard to the hollandaise.

bacon & egg tarts

see base recipe page 170

roasted red pepper & chorizo tarts
Prepare the basic recipe, replacing the bacon with 1 deseeded and chopped roasted red pepper and 125g (4oz) chopped chorizo sausage.

sausage & tomato tarts
Prepare the basic recipe, replacing the bacon with 125g (4oz) chopped sausage and 2 deseeded and chopped fresh tomatoes.

bacon, swiss cheese & onion tarts
Prepare the basic recipe, adding 50g (2oz) grated Gruyère cheese to the tart tins.

mediterranean tarts
Prepare the basic recipe, adding 50g (2oz) chopped sun-dried tomatoes and 50g (2oz) pitted and chopped black olives to the tart tins.

crabmeat tarts
Prepare the basic recipe, omitting the bacon and substituting 125g (4oz) tinned crabmeat, drained. Add 2 teaspoons freshly chopped coriander.

pancakes, waffles & french toast

This is one of my favourite chapters. Pancakes,

waffles and French toast recipes are what I turn to

when giving my grandchildren (and myself!) a

special breakfast treat.

apple pancakes with maple syrup butter

see variations page 201

These are sometimes called German apple pancakes.

125g (4oz) butter, softened
50g (2oz) maple syrup
175g (6oz) flour
2 tbsp rolled oats
2 tbsp wheat bran
½ tsp bicarbonate of soda
2 tsp baking powder
2 tsp sugar

¼ tsp salt
2 large eggs
350ml (12fl.oz) buttermilk
50ml (20fl.oz) whole milk
50g (2oz) butter plus 1 tbsp for cooking
1 Granny Smith apple, peeled, cored
    and thinly sliced
icing sugar, to dust

First make the maple butter. Beat the 125 grams (4 ounces) butter and maple syrup together in an electric mixer until blended. Set aside. In a large bowl, mix all the dry ingredients together. In another bowl, whisk together the eggs, buttermilk and milk. Make a well in the centre of the flour mixture, and pour in the egg mixture. Stir with a wooden spoon from the centre, slowly incorporating the flour from the sides as you stir. Do not overmix or worry about small lumps. In a large frying pan, melt the 50 grams (2 ounces) butter, then tip it into the batter. Put the frying pan back on the heat, add the final 1 tablespoon of butter, swirl it around the pan and, when it is hot, add large spoonfuls of batter to make 13cm (5in) pancakes. Place a few apple slices on top of each pancake and press down into the batter. Cook for about 3 minutes, or until golden, and turn. Cook another 2 minutes. Serve immediately with the apple on top, a dusting of icing sugar, and maple butter on the side.

Makes 10 pancakes

classic blueberry pancakes

see variations page 202

How about starting your day with a fluffy blueberry pancake, spread with butter, sprinkled with icing sugar, and drizzled with delicious maple syrup?

350g (12oz) fresh blueberries
200g (7oz) flour
3 tsp baking powder
2 tsp sugar
good pinch of salt

2 medium eggs
225ml (8fl.oz) milk
1 tsp vanilla extract
50g (2oz) butter, for the batter and cooking
icing sugar, maple syrup and butter, to serve

Heat the oven to 140°C (275°F/Gas mark 1). Divide the blueberries into 8 portions. Sift the dry ingredients into a large bowl. Make a well in the centre, break in the eggs and add the milk and vanilla. Stir from the centre with a wooden spoon, slowly incorporating the flour from the sides as you stir. Do not overmix and do not worry about any lumps. In a large frying pan, melt 2 tablespoons butter, and then tip it into the batter and stir it in lightly. Put the frying pan back on the heat, add a little more butter and swirl it around the base of the pan. When it is nice and hot but not smoking, spoon about 3 tablespoons of batter into the pan to form a pancake about 13cm (5in) in diameter. Spoon in 3 tablespoons more, forming another pancake. Drop a portion of blueberries on top of the pancakes, and press them slightly into the batter. The pancakes should make a sizzling sound and begin to bubble at once. When they look dry at the edges, turn them over. They should have a good brown colour. The second side will cook faster than the first. Place them on a platter, cover, and keep in the warm oven while you make the rest. Serve dusted with icing sugar, with butter and maple syrup on the side.

Makes 8 pancakes

bacon & parsley hotcakes

see variations page 203

Not everyone likes sweet pancakes in the morning. Not only are these pancakes savoury and not sweet, they also have protein in them, which is good for keeping you energised until lunch. They're delicious served with oven-roasted vine tomatoes (see page 254).

8 rashers bacon, finely chopped
75g (3oz) flour
50g (2oz) finely grated Cheddar cheese
1 tsp chopped fresh thyme leaves
2 tbsp chopped fresh parsley

salt and freshly ground black pepper to taste
2 eggs
6 tbsp milk
2 tbsp sunflower oil for frying (or rapeseed oil)

Fry the bacon until crisp and golden, then drain on kitchen towels. In a bowl, mix the flour, cheese, herbs, bacon, salt and pepper. Make a well in the centre, break in the eggs, and add the milk. Stir with a wooden spoon from the centre, slowly incorporating the flour from the sides as you stir. Do not overmix. You should have a fairly thick batter.

In a large frying pan, heat a little sunflower oil. When it is hot, drop in large spoonfuls of the batter. Cook until the hotcakes start to look dry at the edges, then turn them, and cook the other side until golden brown. Keep warm while you make the rest. Serve immediately.

Makes 8 pancakes

chunky monkey pancakes

see variations page 204

Children love the name of these pancakes, and with bananas, chocolate and pecans, they love the taste, too.

200g (7oz) all-purpose flour
3 tsp baking powder
2 tsp sugar
25g (1oz) chopped pecans
good pinch salt
2 small eggs

225ml (8fl.oz) milk
25g (1oz) butter, plus extra for cooking
2 bananas, sliced
175g (6oz) plain chocolate chips
icing sugar, maple syrup and whipped cream to
    serve

Preheat the oven to 140°C (275°F/Gas mark 1). In a large bowl, mix the flour, baking powder, sugar, pecans and salt. Make a well in the centre, break in the eggs and add the milk. Stir with a wooden spoon from the centre, slowly incorporating the flour from the sides as you stir. Do not overmix.

Melt the butter in a large frying pan, then stir it into the batter. Add a little more butter to the pan, and when the pan is hot, drop in large spoonfuls of batter to make 13cm (5in) pancakes. Drop a few slices of banana and some chocolate chips onto each pancake, pressing them into the batter slightly. They should make a sizzling sound and begin to bubble at once. When they look dry at the edges, turn them over. They should have a good brown colour. The second side will cook faster than the first. Place pancakes on a platter and keep warm while you make the rest. Serve with a dusting of icing sugar, maple syrup and whipped cream.

Makes 10 pancakes

stuffed savoury ham & cheese french toast

see variations page 205

Butter burns easily when heated — add a little vegetable oil and it will not burn so readily.

125g (4oz) cream cheese, softened
125g (4oz) grated Cheddar cheese
2 spring onions, finely chopped
salt and freshly ground black pepper, to taste
4 slices ham
8 thick slices day-old white bread

4 eggs
125ml (4fl.oz) milk
few shakes of hot sauce, to taste
butter and vegetable oil, for cooking
icing sugar and maple syrup, to serve

In a medium bowl, mix the cream cheese and Cheddar with the spring onions. Season with salt and pepper. Spread 4 slices of bread generously with the filling, lay a slice of ham on top of each one and top with the remaining bread slices, making 4 sandwiches.

In a shallow dish, whisk together the eggs, milk, salt, pepper and hot sauce. Dip each sandwich in the batter, turning to coat both sides, and allowing each side to soak up some of the batter. Do not soak too long or the sandwiches will fall apart when you lift them.

In a large frying pan, heat a little butter and vegetable oil. When it is good and hot, lay 1 or 2 sandwiches in the frying pan, and cook them to a rich brown. Turn and cook the other side. Keep warm while you make the rest. Serve immediately, with a sprinkling of icing sugar and with maple syrup on the side.

Serves 4

almond waffles with apricot sauce

see variations page 206

Almonds and apricots are a classic combination, and the buttermilk gives a lovely tangy richness to this waffle.

for the apricot sauce
1 (450g/lb) can apricots
300g (11oz) brown sugar

for the waffles
175g (6oz) flour
1 tsp bicarbonate of soda
2 tsp baking powder

½ tsp salt
2 tbsp sugar
50g (2oz) finely chopped almonds
425ml (14fl.oz) buttermilk
1 tsp almond extract
25g (1oz) butter, melted, plus more for cooking
3 eggs, separated
icing sugar, to serve

First make the apricot sauce. Strain the apricots, reserving the juice. Chop the apricots. Place the apricots, juice and brown sugar in a medium saucepan over medium heat. Bring to the boil and simmer for 5–6 minutes. Preheat the waffle iron. In a large bowl, sift together the flour, bicarbonate of soda, baking powder, salt and sugar. Stir in the almonds. In another bowl, beat together the buttermilk, almond extract, 2 tablespoons cooled melted butter and egg yolks. Stir the flour mixture into the milk mixture, and beat well to make a smooth batter. In a clean bowl, whisk the egg whites until stiff peaks form, then gently fold them into the batter with a metal spoon. Do not overmix. Once your waffle iron is hot, brush with a little butter, and spoon in enough batter to just cover the base. Remember the batter will rise and spread during cooking. Cook until crisp and golden, about 3–4 minutes. Keep warm while you make the rest, then serve immediately, sprinkled with a little icing sugar, with the apricot sauce on the side.

Makes 8 large waffles

cheddar & mushroom crêpes

see variations page 207

The crêpe is a wonderfully versatile pancake to serve at any time of day, and you can fill it with so many different ingredients. This is a favourite recipe.

1 tbsp vegetable oil
225g (8oz) sliced button mushrooms
50g (2oz) grated Cheddar cheese,
    plus extra to garnish

for the batter
125g (4oz) plain flour
pinch salt
1 large egg, lightly beaten
300ml (10fl.oz) milk
oil, for brushing
chopped fresh parsley, to garnish

Heat the oven to 190°C (375°F/Gas mark 5) and grease the base and sides of a casserole dish. In a medium saucepan, heat the oil and add the mushrooms. Sauté for about 7 minutes until all the liquid has come out. Drain on a kitchen towel, then place in a bowl. Set aside.

To make the crêpes, sift the flour and salt into a large bowl. Using a wooden spoon, make a well in the centre, and break in the egg. Gradually add half the milk, stirring from the centre, and slowly incorporate the flour from the sides as you stir. When all the flour is mixed in, beat the mixture with the wooden spoon or an electric mixer, until it becomes smooth and free of lumps. Allow the batter to stand for a few minutes, then add the remainder of the milk, beating continuously, until the batter is bubbly and has a smooth consistency.

Heat a nonstick frying pan, and brush lightly with oil. The pan should be really hot before you add the batter. Using a small jug or a ladle, pour in just enough batter to flow in a thin film over the base, tilting the pan to spread it. The heat is right if the underside of the crêpe

becomes golden in 1 minute. Using a palette knife, flip the crêpe over and cook the other side. Keep warm while you make the rest. Mix the cooled mushrooms with the cheese and divide between all 8 crêpes, folding the sides over to encase the filling.

Place side by side in the greased casserole dish and top with extra grated cheese. Bake for just 5 minutes to melt the cheese. Serve immediately, sprinkled with parsley.

Serves 4

chocolate chip waffles

see variations page 208

The smell of these cooking will get everyone out of bed in double-quick time.

for the chocolate sauce
300ml (10fl.oz) double cream
225g (8oz) plain chocolate, broken into pieces
1 tbsp golden syrup

for the waffles
175g (6oz) flour
1½ tsp baking powder
2 tbsp sugar

75g (3oz) plain chocolate chips
½ tsp salt
300ml (10fl.oz) milk
2 large eggs
60g (2½oz) butter, melted, plus extra for
    cooking
icing sugar, to serve

To make the chocolate sauce, heat the cream in a medium saucepan until almost boiling. Add the chocolate and golden syrup, and stir until the chocolate has melted and the sauce is smooth and creamy. Serve hot or cold.

Preheat the waffle iron. In a large bowl, using a fork, mix together the flour, baking powder, sugar, chocolate chips and salt. In another bowl, whisk the milk and eggs together, then pour into the flour mixture. Mix together with the fork until there are no large lumps, but do not overmix. Stir in the 5 tablespoons melted butter. When the iron is hot, lightly brush it with some melted butter, then spoon in enough batter to just cover the base. Remember the batter will rise and spread during cooking. Cook for 3–5 minutes, until crisp. Keep warm while you make the rest. Serve immediately, sprinkled with a little icing sugar and with the chocolate sauce on the side.

Makes 8 waffles

bacon waffles with sausage gravy

see variations page 209

Sausage gravy is a southern American classic usually served over scone-like biscuits.

for the bacon
10 rashers bacon
25g (1oz) brown sugar

for the sausage gravy
450g (1lb) pork sausage, crumbled
2 tbsp finely chopped onion
1 tbsp vegetable oil
5 tbsp flour
700ml (1¼ pints) milk
1 or 2 chicken stock cubes, crumbled
½ tsp freshly chopped sage
salt and freshly ground black pepper to taste

for the waffles
175g flour
1½ tsp baking powder
2 tbsp sugar
½ tsp salt
2 large eggs
300ml (10fl.oz) milk
40g (1½oz) butter, melted, plus extra
    for cooking

Prepare the bacon. Preheat the oven to 190˚C (375˚F/Gas mark 5) and line a baking tray with foil. Grease the foil with a little vegetable oil and arrange the bacon rashers in a single layer on top. Sprinkle generously with brown sugar and bake in the top of the oven until the bacon is crisp and the sugar is caramelised, about 10-15 minutes. Remove from the oven and place the bacon on a cutting board (not on kitchen towels). When cool, chop very small.

To make gravy, in a large frying pan, fry sausage and onion in a little oil until brown and cooked through. Drain off all but 2-3 tablespoons fat. Stir in the flour until blended. Cook for 2 or 3 minutes, and gradually add the milk, stirring continually, until it thickens into a sauce. Crumble in the stock cubes, and season with salt and pepper. Cover and keep warm.

To make the waffles, preheat waffle iron. Mix all the dry ingredients in a large bowl. In another bowl, whisk the eggs and milk, then pour into the dry ingredients. Using a fork, fold together very lightly until there are no large lumps. Stir in the bacon bits. Do not overmix. Pour in the melted butter, and give one last stir.

When the waffle iron is hot, lightly brush it with a little butter and spoon in enough batter to just cover the base. Remember the batter will spread and rise during cooking. Cook for 3–5 minutes until waffle is crisp and golden. Keep warm while you make the rest. Serve immediately with gravy on the side.

Makes 10 waffles

apple & pecan french toast

see variations page 210

This is a great way to use up leftover panettone or brioche, but any type of day-old white bread will be good (day-old bread is always better than fresh for French toast).

50g (2oz) butter
50g (2oz) sugar
2 tsp vanilla extract
½ tsp ground cinnamon
pinch salt
¼ tsp ground nutmeg
4 apples, peeled, cored and chopped
4 large eggs
3 tbsp molasses or black treacle

125ml (4fl.oz) double cream
½ tsp ground cinnamon
½ tsp ground ginger
pinch salt
12 slices day-old white bread (or panettone, challah or brioche)
butter and a little vegetable oil, for cooking
125g (4oz) chopped pecans
sprinkling of icing sugar, to serve

In a large saucepan, combine the butter, sugar, half the vanilla, cinnamon, salt and nutmeg, and heat until sizzling. Lower the heat, and add the chopped apples. Simmer gently, stirring, until the apples are very tender and the sauce thickens and browns, about 15 minutes. Add a little water if the mixture begins to burn. Set aside to cool slightly. In a shallow dish, whisk the eggs, molasses, cream, remaining vanilla, cinnamon, ginger and salt. Dip each slice of bread into the mixture, coating both sides, and arrange the slices in a pyramid on a plate. Melt a little butter and vegetable oil in a large frying pan. When it is hot but not smoking, put in the bread slices and sprinkle a few chopped pecans on top. Press pecans lightly into the bread, and cook to a rich brown. Turn the toast and cook the other side, shaking the pan slightly to make sure it does not stick. Remove and keep warm while you make the rest. Serve immediately with a sprinkling of powdered sugar and caramelised apples on the side.

Serves 6

overnight caramel pecan french toast

see variations page 211

Start this the night before, and it will be ready to bake in the morning. It's easy, but never fails to impress!

225g (8oz) brown sugar
125g (4oz) butter
2 tbsp golden syrup
125g (4oz) chopped pecans
18 (1cm/½cm thick) slices day-old French bread
6 eggs, beaten

350ml (12fl.oz) milk
1 tsp vanilla extract
1 tbsp sugar
1½ tsp ground cinnamon
½ tsp ground nutmeg

For the caramel, mix together the brown sugar, butter and golden syrup in a medium saucepan. Heat and stir until the butter is melted and the brown sugar dissolved. Pour into an ungreased 23x33-cm (9x13-in) rectangular baking dish and sprinkle with half the pecans. Arrange half of the bread slices in a single layer on top of the caramel, sprinkle with the rest of the pecans, and top with the remaining bread slices. In a medium bowl, whisk together the eggs, milk and vanilla, and carefully pour over the bread. Press lightly with the back of a spoon to moisten the bread. In a small bowl, mix together the sugar, cinnamon, and nutmeg, and sprinkle over the bread. Cover and chill for 8–24 hours.

Preheat the oven to 175°C (350°F/Gas mark 4) Remove the cover, and bake for 30–40 minutes, until lightly browned. Leave to stand for 10 minutes. To serve, remove individual portions with a spatula and invert onto serving plates. Dust with icing sugar, and provide maple syrup on the side.

Serves 9

variations

apple pancakes with maple syrup butter

see base recipe page 183

apple & walnut pancakes with maple syrup butter
Prepare the basic recipe, adding 25g (1oz) chopped walnuts to the dry ingredients.

pear pancakes with maple syrup butter
Prepare the basic recipe, replacing the apple with slices of pear.

apple & cinnamon pancakes with maple syrup butter
Prepare the basic recipe, adding 2 teaspoons cinnamon to the dry ingredients.

apricot pancakes with maple syrup butter
Prepare the basic recipe, replacing the apple with slices of apricot.

apple & raisin pancakes with maple syrup butter
Prepare the basic recipe, adding 50g (2oz) raisins to the dry ingredients.

variations

classic blueberry pancakes

see base recipe page 184

classic raspberry & almond pancakes
Prepare the basic recipe, replacing the blueberries with raspberries and the vanilla extract with almond extract.

classic strawberry & white chocolate pancakes
Prepare the basic recipe, replacing the blueberries with hulled and chopped strawberries and 50g (2oz) white chocolate chips.

classic peaches & cream pancakes
Prepare the basic recipe, replacing the blueberries with chopped fresh or canned peaches. Serve the pancakes with a swirl of whipped cream.

classic cherry & almond pancakes
Prepare the basic recipe, replacing the blueberries with pitted and chopped cherries and the vanilla extract with almond extract.

classic gingerbread blueberry pancakes
Prepare the basic recipe, replacing 1 tablespoon milk with 1 tablespoon molasses or treacle and adding 1 tablespoon ground ginger to the mixture.

variations

bacon & parsley hotcakes

see base recipe page 187

bacon, parsley & pine nut hotcakes
Prepare the basic recipe, adding 50g (2oz) pine nuts to the dry ingredients.

bacon, parsley & poppy seed hotcakes
Prepare the basic recipe, adding 2 tablespoons poppy seeds to the
dry ingredients.

bacon, parsley & oatmeal hotcakes
Prepare the basic recipe, replacing 2 tablespoons flour with 2 tablespoons
rolled oats.

bacon, parsley & tomato hotcakes
Prepare the basic recipe, adding 1 tomato, deseeded and chopped, to the
wet ingredients.

bacon, parsley & Gruyère hotcakes
Prepare the basic recipe, replacing the Cheddar cheese with Gruyère.

variations

chunky monkey pancakes

see base recipe page 188

white chocolate chunky monkey pancakes with raspberries
Prepare the basic recipe, replacing the plain chocolate chips with white
chocolate chips. Replace half the banana with fresh raspberries.

praline chunky monkey pancakes
Prepare the basic recipe, replacing the plain chocolate chips with crushed
praline. Serve with caramelised apple topping (page 198).

coconut chunky monkey pancakes with raspberry coulis
Prepare the basic recipe, adding 25g (1oz) desiccated coconut to the dry
ingredients. Serve with a raspberry coulis, made by pressing 225g (8oz) fresh
raspberries through a sieve into a medium bowl. Add 3 tablespoons sifted
icing sugar, or to taste, and stir until smooth.

double chocolate chunky monkey pancakes with chocolate sauce
Prepare the basic recipe, replacing half the plain chocolate chips with white
chocolate chips. Serve with chocolate sauce (page 195).

variations

stuffed savoury ham & cheese french toast

see base recipe page 190

stuffed savoury ham, cheese & mushroom french toast
Prepare the basic recipe, adding a few sliced cooked button mushrooms to the filling. Replace the topping with a sprinkle of paprika, just before serving.

stuffed savoury cheese, onion & and pesto french toast
Prepare the basic recipe, omitting the ham and adding a teaspoon of basil pesto to each sandwich filling. Replace the topping with a sprinkle of freshly chopped parsley before serving.

stuffed savoury ham, mustard & gruyère french toast
Prepare the basic recipe, replacing the Cheddar cheese with Gruyère cheese. Spread a teaspoon of Dijon mustard on top of each ham slice before topping with the bread slice. Replace the topping with a little freshly chopped coriander before serving.

stuffed savoury cheese & tomato french toast
Prepare the basic recipe, omitting the ham and adding thinly sliced plum tomatoes. Replace the topping with a sprinkle of grated Cheddar cheese before serving.

almond waffles with apricot sauce

see base recipe page 191

georgia waffles
Prepare the basic recipe, replacing the almonds with chopped pecans and the apricots with chopped canned peaches.

lemon poppy seed waffles with raspberry sauce
Prepare the basic recipe, replacing the almonds with 1 tablespoon grated lemon peel and 1 tablespoon poppy seeds. Make a raspberry sauce by mixing 3 tablespoons sugar with 1 tablespoon cornflour in a medium saucepan. Stir in 175ml (6fl.oz) orange juice and 125g (4oz) tinned raspberries in syrup. Over medium heat, cook, stirring, until the mixture boils and thickens. Simmer for 1 minute, then remove and let cool slightly.

orange pecan waffles with butter pecan syrup
Prepare the basic recipe, replacing the almonds with chopped pecans and 1 tablespoon grated orange peel. For the topping, melt 25g (1oz) butter over medium heat, and add 25g (1oz) chopped pecans. Cook until they are browned, stirring constantly, and stir in 175g (6oz) maple-flavoured syrup. When hot, remove from the heat and leave to cool slightly before serving.

cheddar & mushroom crêpes

see base recipe page 192

edam & mushroom crêpes
Prepare the basic recipe, replacing the Cheddar cheese with Edam cheese.

gruyère cheese & corn crêpes
Prepare the basic recipe, omitting the oil and replacing the Cheddar cheese with Gruyère and the mushrooms with 125g (4oz) sweetcorn kernels.

cheddar, stilton & squash crêpes
Prepare the basic recipe, omitting the oil and replacing the mushrooms with 225g (8oz) chopped roasted butternut squash. Add 50g (2oz) Stilton cheese, crumbled, to the filling.

cheddar & mushroom crêpes with brie & bacon
Prepare the basic recipe, adding 50g (2oz) sliced brie and 6 rashers crisp bacon, broken into bite-size pieces, to the filling.

cheddar & mushroom crêpes with cream cheese & chives
Prepare the basic recipe, adding 125g (4oz) cream cheese and 2 tablespoons freshly chopped chives to the filling.

variations

chocolate chip waffles

see base recipe page 195

chocolate chip & banana waffles with amaretto chocolate sauce
Prepare the basic waffles, adding 1 mashed ripe banana to the wet
ingredients. Add 1 tablespoon amaretto to the sauce.

**chocolate chip & peanut butter waffles with honey peanut
butter syrup**
Prepare the basic waffles, adding 50g (2oz) peanut butter, loosened with
a little double cream, to the wet ingredients. For the syrup, over low heat,
mix 225g (8oz) honey and 125g (4oz) peanut butter, stirring until smooth
and warm.

chocolate chip & strawberry waffles with strawberry sauce
Prepare the basic waffles, adding 50g (2oz) chopped strawberries. For
the sauce, mix 1 tablespoon cornflour with 3 tablespoons sugar and
125ml (4fl.oz) orange juice. Over medium heat, add 450g (1lb) chopped
strawberries, 2 tablespoons strawberry jam, and 1 tablespoon golden syrup.
Heat gently until boiling, stirring. Simmer for a minute or two,
or until berries have broken down and sauce is thickened.

variations

bacon waffles with sausage gravy

see base recipe page 196

sun-dried tomato & basil waffles with italian sausage gravy
Prepare the basic recipe, omitting the bacon and substituting 75g (3oz)
chopped, sun-dried tomatoes and 1 tablespoon grated fresh basil leaves.
Prepare the sausage gravy with Italian sausage.

pine nut & poppy seed waffles with sausage gravy
Prepare the basic recipe, replacing the bacon with 25g (1oz) pine nuts and
1 tablespoon poppy seeds.

bacon, cheese & chive waffles with sausage gravy
Prepare the basic recipe, adding 25g (1oz) finely grated Parmesan cheese
and 2 tablespoons freshly chopped chives to the dry ingredients.

turkey waffles with sausage gravy
Prepare the basic recipe, replacing the bacon with turkey rashers.

variations

apple & pecan french toast

see base recipe page 198

walnut french toast with caramelised apples & raisins
Prepare the basic recipe, replacing the pecans with walnuts. For the topping, add 2 tablespoons raisins to the apples during cooking.

citrus–pecan french toast with lemon topping
Prepare the basic recipe, adding the grated zest of 1 orange to the custard. Instead of the apples, place 1 or 2 tablespoons canned lemon pie filling or lemon curd on top of each portion, and add a swirl of whipped cream, if desired.

cinnamon–pecan french toast with caramelised apples
Prepare the basic recipe, adding an extra 2 teaspoons ground cinnamon to the dry ingredients.

brandy french toast with caramelised apples & walnuts
Prepare the basic recipe, adding 2 tablespoons brandy to the custard. For the topping, add 2 tablespoons chopped walnuts to the apples during cooking.

honey–pecan french toast with caramelised apples & pears
Prepare the basic recipe, adding 2 tablespoons honey to the custard. For the topping, replace half the apples with pears.

variations

overnight caramel pecan french toast

see base recipe page 200

overnight caramel, raspberry & almond french toast
Prepare the basic recipe, replacing the pecans with almonds. Scatter
125g (4oz) fresh raspberries on the first layer of bread in the dish, and
sprinkle 1 tablespoon flaked almonds over the top before chilling. Garnish
each serving with a few fresh raspberries.

overnight caramel, peach & pecan french toast
Prepare the basic recipe, scattering 125g (4oz) peeled and chopped fresh
peaches on the first layer of bread in the dish. Add a few slices of peeled
and sliced fresh peaches to each serving.

overnight caramel, banana & walnut french toast
Prepare the basic recipe, replacing the pecans with walnuts. Add 2 sliced
bananas to the first layer of bread in the dish.

overnight caramel, chocolate & pecan french toast
Prepare the basic recipe, adding 50g (2oz) chocolate chips to the first layer of
bread in the dish. Just before serving, sprinkle with grated plain chocolate.

big plates

Savour a long, chatty, weekend breakfast with big plates of eggs, meat, potatoes and toast. Whatever your style, this chapter gives you abundant filling ideas to start your day.

kedgeree

see variations page 225

This is a traditional breakfast dish of Indian origin. It originally consisted of rice, onion, lentils, spices, fresh limes, butter and fish.

butter, for greasing
2 hard-boiled eggs
450g (1lb) smoked fish, preferably haddock
900g (2lb) boiled rice
¼ tsp ground nutmeg

2 tsp freshly chopped parsley
salt and freshly ground black pepper
50ml (2fl.oz) whipping cream
50g (2oz) butter

Preheat the oven to 180°C (350°F/Gas mark 4) and liberally butter a deep baking dish.

Cut the eggs into small wedges. Flake the fish into a medium bowl. Add the rice, nutmeg and parsley and season with salt and pepper. Pour in the cream, add the eggs and stir together lightly. Tip into the baking dish and dot with butter. Cover the dish with a lid and bake for about 30 minutes, until heated through. Serve immediately.

Serves 4

the great british fry-up

see variations page 226

This is an iconic breakfast, enjoyed by the British all around the world. Why not try making your own baked beans, using the smoky beans recipe on page 251.

vegetable oil, for cooking
8 pork sausages, the best you can buy (or make your own, recipe page 249)
8 rashers back bacon (or 12 rashers bacon)
1 (450g/1lb) tin baked beans (or smoky beans, page 265)

225g (8oz) sliced button mushrooms
4 ripe tomatoes, halved
toast or hash browns (page 258)
4 eggs

Heat the oven to 140°C (275°F/Gas mark 1). In a large frying pan, heat a little vegetable oil. When it is hot, put in the sausages and cook them slowly, over a medium heat, for about 20 minutes until browned, turning them occasionally. Remove the sausages from the frying pan and keep warm in the oven. Place the bacon in the frying pan and fry for 2-4 minutes on each side until crisp and browned. Remove and keep warm in the oven. Heat baked beans slowly in a small saucepan while you cook the rest of the meal, stirring occasionally.

Increase the heat under the frying pan and add the mushrooms. Cook, without stirring, for a few minutes, and when browned, remove from frying pan and keep warm in the oven. Place tomatoes cut-side down in the frying pan. Cook for 2 minutes on medium heat, gently turn over, and cook the other side for 2 minutes, until tender. Remove from frying pan and keep warm in the oven. Prepare toast or warm hash-browns. The eggs are the last to cook and are best if served immediately. At this stage, place all the other ingredients onto serving plates and put back into the oven to keep warm.

Break an egg into a small bowl. Clean the frying pan, add 3 or 4 tablespoons vegetable oil, and when it is hot, carefully tip in the egg. If the frying pan is big enough, cook all 4 at once. Cook slowly, basting with the hot oil, until the white is cooked and the yolk is hot, or until it is cooked as you like it. You can flip it over if you prefer it over-easy. Once done, remove from the frying pan immediately, add to the other items on the plates, and serve.

Serves 4

sausage & onion rosti

see variations page 227

This is an unusual way of serving rosti (a Swiss version of hash browns), with meaty sausages, browned and baked in the oven.

butter, for greasing
3 tbsp olive oil
1 small onion, finely chopped
4 large peeled potatoes

8 sausages, the best you can buy, or make your own (page 249)
2 tbsp freshly chopped parsley, to serve

Preheat the oven to 190°C (375°F/Gas mark 5) and grease a nonstick 32x23-cm (9x13-in) rectangular metal roasting pan with butter. Heat 1 tablespoon olive oil in a small frying pan, add the onion, and fry over medium heat for 6-8 minutes, until softened and lightly browned. Set aside.

Grate the potatoes into a sieve. Rinse with water, drain well, place in a tea towel and squeeze out as much water as possible. Spread the remaining oil in the roasting pan, add the potatoes, and bake for 10 minutes. Remove from the oven, scatter the onion on top, and place the sausages on top, evenly spaced. Bake for 20 minutes, then turn the sausages over.

Bake for 20 minutes more, or until the rosti is brown and crispy and so are the sausages. Serve immediately. Cut the rosti into quarters and place on serving plates, with 2 sausages each, and scatter the parsley over the top.

Serves 4

tex-mex sausage bake

see variations page 228

This will fill your kitchen with the wonderful aroma of cheese as it bakes in the oven. You can increase the "heat" of this dish by using jalapeño peppers and/or pepper jack cheese, if you wish.

450g (1lb) pork sausage, crumbled
6 spring onions, chopped
1 red pepper, deseeded and chopped
25g (1oz) finely chopped mild green chillies
450g (1lb) cooked 5mm (¼in) potato cubes
350g (12oz) finely chopped mozzarella

4 eggs
175ml (6fl.oz) milk
salt and freshly ground black pepper
pinch cayenne pepper
few shakes of Tabasco sauce
grated Parmesan cheese, for sprinkling

Heat the oven to 190°C (375°F/Gas mark 5) and grease a large baking dish. In a large frying pan, cook the sausage for a few minutes until it starts to brown. Drain on paper towels. Put back into the frying pan and add the spring onions, pepper and chillies. Fry until the sausage has cooked and the pepper has softened. In the baking dish, layer half the potatoes, half the cheese and all the cooked sausage mixture. Top with the remaining potatoes and then the remaining cheese.

In a medium bowl, whisk the eggs and the milk together, then season with salt, pepper, cayenne pepper and hot sauce to taste. Pour evenly over the mixture in the baking dish. Cover with a lid or foil that has been buttered so it does not stick. Bake for 60 minutes. Remove lid or foil, sprinkle top with Parmesan cheese, and bake for 10 minutes more, or until a knife inserted in the centre comes out clean. Let it stand for 10 minutes before serving, cut into wedges.
Serves 6

corned beef hash with poached eggs

see variations page 229

I like this corned beef hash recipe because it's very well flavoured. Try to keep the corned beef in chunks, rather than letting it cook down to a mash, so you can taste the different textures.

butter, for greasing
4 large potatoes, unpeeled, cut into cubes
3 tbsp olive oil
1 onion, sliced
1 (350g/12oz) tin corned beef, cut into chunks
4 tbsp Worcestershire sauce

1 large pickled gherkin, chopped
2 tsp whole-grain mustard
salt and freshly ground black pepper
2 tbsp freshly chopped parsley
4 poached eggs (see page 155), to serve

Preheat the grill and grease a large baking dish generously with butter. In a large saucepan, boil the potato cubes for 5 minutes, then drain. In a large frying pan, heat 2 tablespoons olive oil and fry the onion for a few minutes until softened and lightly browned. In a medium bowl, gently mix the corned beef chunks, onion, Worcestershire sauce, chopped gherkin, mustard, salt and pepper and parsley.

In the frying pan, heat the remaining oil, and fry the potatoes until they are tender and just starting to brown at the edges. Place the corned beef mixture in the baking dish and top with the potatoes. Place the dish under the grill and cook until the top is crisp and golden brown, about 5-6 minutes. Serve immediately, topping each serving with a poached egg.

Serves 4

meat lovers' potato frying pan

see variations page 230

If you'd like, you can cook the potatoes the night before, then cook this one-pan meal in the morning. It's filling and satisfying. Serve it by itself or as a side dish for eggs.

700g (1½lb) 5mm (¼in) peeled potato cubes
2 tbsp vegetable oil, plus extra if required
1 medium onion, chopped
125g (4oz) chopped spicy chorizo

125g (4oz) chopped crisply cooked bacon
125g (4oz) ham cut into strips
salt and freshly ground black pepper
2 tbsp freshly chopped parsley, to serve

In a large saucepan, cook the cubed potatoes in boiling water for 5 minutes, then remove and drain well.

In a large frying pan, heat 2 tablespoons vegetable oil over medium heat, then fry the onion for a few minutes until it has softened. Turn the heat to medium-high and add the potatoes to the frying pan. Fry until they are crispy at the edges, adding more oil if necessary. Stir continuously until they are browned all over, then add all the meat. Season well with salt and pepper. Keep turning the mixture around the pan until the meat is heated through. Add chopped parsley and serve immediately.

Serves 4-5

ham, cheese & bacon tartiflette

see variations page 231

A tartiflette is a hot, bubbling dish with cheese and onion, originating in France. There, the cheese used is Reblochon, which may be difficult to find at the supermarket.

50g (2oz) unsalted butter, plus extra for
    greasing
1.1kg (2½lb) potatoes, peeled and roughly
    chopped
1 onion, chopped
2 garlic cloves, finely chopped
1 tbsp fresh thyme leaves

10 rashers bacon, chopped
125ml (4fl.oz) dry white wine
225ml (8fl.oz) double cream
125g (4oz) ham, cut into strips
175g (6oz) grated Gruyère cheese
salt and freshly ground black pepper

Preheat the oven to 200°C (400°F/Gas mark 6), and grease a large baking dish generously with butter. In a large saucepan, boil the potatoes for 5 minutes, then drain. In a large frying pan, melt the 50g (2oz) butter over medium heat. Add the onion and fry for a few minutes until softened and lightly browned. Add the garlic, thyme and chopped bacon, and cook for 5 minutes, stirring constantly. Stir in the wine, cream, ham, potatoes and most of the cheese. Season with salt and pepper. Transfer to the baking dish and cover with a lid or foil that has been oiled to prevent it sticking. Bake for 20 minutes, then remove the lid or foil, sprinkle on the remaining cheese, and bake for 20 minutes more, or until bubbling and golden brown.

Serves 4

variations

kedgeree

see base recipe page 213

smoky kedgeree
Prepare the basic recipe, adding 2 teaspoons smoked paprika to the rice mixture.

kedgeree with bacon
Prepare the basic recipe, adding 2 rashers cooked and crispy bacon to the
rice mixture.

kedgeree with mushrooms
Prepare the basic recipe, adding 100g (4oz) cooked and sliced button
mushrooms to the rice mixture.

kedgeree with sausages
Prepare the basic recipe, adding 2 cooked and sliced chipolatas to the
rice mixture.

kedgeree with a hint of curry
Prepare the basic recipe, adding 2 teaspoons curry powder to the rice mixture.

variations

the great british fry-up

see base recipe page 214

great british fry-up with fried bread
Prepare the basic recipe, replacing toast or hash browns with fried bread. To make it, quickly fry thick slices of white bread in very hot vegetable oil until crispy on both sides.

fry-up with fried green tomatoes
Prepare the basic recipe, omitting the tomatoes. Replace with fried green tomatoes, made by dipping unripened green tomato slices into semolina, seasoned with salt and pepper, and frying in a little oil or bacon fat.

vegetarian fry-up
Prepare the basic recipe, omitting all meat. Serve with a stuffed red pepper, made by cutting pepper in half lengthwise, and stuffing both halves with cooked rice mixed with chopped spring onion and fresh parsley, and sprinkled with a little grated Cheddar cheese. Bake on a greased pan for 15 minutes at 180°C (350°F/Gas mark 4).

pork chop fry-up
Prepare the basic recipe, replacing the sausages with a grilled or roasted pork chop.

variations

sausage & onion rosti

see base recipe page 217

sausage & onion rosti with bacon
Prepare the basic recipe, adding 2 rashers chopped bacon to the frying pan with the onion.

sausage & onion rosti with cheese
Prepare the basic recipe, sprinkling 50g (2oz) grated Cheddar cheese on top of the sausages and rosti 10 minutes before the end of cooking time.

sausage & onion rosti with mushrooms
Prepare the basic recipe, scattering 100g (4oz) cooked and sliced button mushrooms on top of the sausages and rosti 10 minutes before the end of cooking time.

sausage & onion rosti with chile
Prepare the basic recipe, adding 1 finely chopped mild green chile to the frying pan with the onion.

variations

tex-mex sausage bake

see base recipe page 218

tex-mex sausage bake with bacon
Prepare the basic recipe, adding 4 rashers chopped bacon to the frying pan with the onions.

tex-mex sausage bake with corn
Prepare the basic recipe, adding 1 (415-g/15-oz) can sweetcorn, drained, to the baking dish with the layers.

tex-mex sausage bake with mushrooms
Prepare the basic recipe, adding 100g (4oz) sliced button mushrooms to the frying pan with the onion.

tex-mex sausage bake with spicy chilli beans
Prepare the basic recipe, adding 1 (400-g/15-oz) can spicy chilli beans to the layers in the baking dish.

tex-mex sausage bake with corned beef
Prepare the basic recipe, replacing the sausage with corned beef.

corned beef hash with poached eggs

see base recipe page 220

corned beef hash with cheese & poached eggs
Prepare the basic recipe, sprinkling 50g (2oz) grated Cheddar cheese over the potatoes just before grilling.

corned beef hash with peppers & poached eggs
Prepare the basic recipe, adding 1 red pepper, seeded and sliced, to the frying pan with the corned beef.

corned beef hash with mushrooms & poached eggs
Prepare the basic recipe, adding 100g (4oz) sliced button mushrooms to the frying pan with the onion.

corned beef hash with corn & poached eggs
Prepare the basic recipe, adding 1 (15-oz.) can sweetcorn to the frying pan with the corned beef.

corned beef hash with bacon & poached eggs
Prepare the basic recipe, sprinkling 2 rashers cooked and crumbled crisp bacon over the potatoes and topping with 50g (2oz) grated Cheddar cheese just before grilling.

variations

meat lovers' potato frying pan

see base recipe page 223

meat lovers' sweet potato frying pan
Prepare the basic recipe, replacing half the potatoes with sweet potatoes.

meat lovers' potato & corn frying pan
Prepare the basic recipe, adding 1 (400-g/15-oz) can sweetcorn, drained, to the frying pan with the salt and pepper.

meat lovers' potato & chile frying pan
Prepare the basic recipe, adding 1 mild green chilli, finely chopped, to the frying pan with the onion.

meat lovers' potato & tomato frying pan
Prepare the basic recipe, adding 3 seeded and chopped tomatoes to the frying pan with the salt and pepper.

meat lovers' potato & pepper frying pan
Prepare the basic recipe, adding 1 green pepper, seeded and sliced, to the frying pan with the onion.

ham, cheese & bacon tartiflette

see base recipe page 224

ham, cheese & pancetta tartiflette
Prepare the basic recipe, replacing the bacon with chopped pancetta.

parma ham, cheese & bacon tartiflette
Prepare the basic recipe, replacing the ham with parma ham.

chorizo, cheese & bacon tartiflette
Prepare the basic recipe, replacing the ham with chopped chorizo.

ham, cheese, bacon & corn tartiflette
Prepare the basic recipe, adding 1 (400-g/15-oz) can sweetcorn, drained, to the frying pan with the potatoes.

ham, cheese & bacon tartiflette with garlic
Prepare the basic recipe, adding 1 crushed garlic clove to the frying pan with the onion.

sides &
sandwiches

When you're hosting a holiday brunch, you'll want
to include some of these hearty and delicious side
dishes. Sausages, glazed ham steak, oven-roasted
tomatoes and hash browns will add the crowning
touch to your buffet table. Or grab a breakfast
calzone or burrito and dash off to work.

homemade pork sausages

see variations page 265

Making sausages is much easier than most people think. Sausage skins can quite often be purchased from butchers who make their own sausages. Alternatively, just roll into a sausage shape, and cut into sections about 10cm (4in) in length. You could also form the sausage meat into patties and cook them like a burger, easy to put on a sausage sandwich. These can be frozen until needed; just defrost completely before cooking.

2.3kg (5lb) minced pork
2 tsp ground white pepper
1 tsp ground ginger
1 tsp ground sage

1 tsp ground mace
3 tbsp salt
225g (8oz) fresh breadcrumbs
3 metres (10 ft) hog casing, rinsed and drained

In a large bowl, using your hands, combine all the ingredients (not the casings) together, making sure that the herbs and spices are distributed evenly.

If you have a sausage stuffer on a freestanding tabletop mixer, thread the hog casings onto the stuffer. You will find it easier to stuff the casings with two people, one to push the meat through and one to guide the casing off the stuffer, ensuring there is an even distribution of meat in the casing. This helps keep the sausages the same size. Keep going until you have used up all the meat. You can double the ingredients to make twice the number of sausages, if you can manage that amount. Twist sausages into links and store in refrigerator. Alternatively, after mixing the sausage, roll out on a floured work surface into a sausage shape and cut into sections about 10cm (4in) in length. If not using immediately, store in the refrigerator. Keep for up to 1 week in the refrigerator or 3 months in the freezer.

Makes just over 5 pounds

gammon with pineapple salsa

see variations page 266

Gammon is a popular ham in England, and this recipe is gammon (ham steaks are a fine substitute) and pineapple with a twist. You can use fresh or canned pineapple for the salsa, but fresh is best.

for the pineapple salsa
2 tbsp brown sugar
2 tbsp soy sauce
450g (1lb) finely chopped pineapple
    (preferably fresh)
1 red chilli pepper, deseeded and finely chopped
3 tbsp freshly chopped coriander

for the ham
2 large or 4 small thick gammon or ham steaks,
    rind on
2 tbsp vegetable oil, for brushing and greasing
3 tsp honey

First make the salsa. In a medium bowl, mix the soy sauce and the brown sugar together, and then add the rest of the ingredients. Mix well and set aside.

Preheat the grill and grease a baking tray with a little oil. If you have large ham steaks, slice them in half so you have 4 portions. Carefully snip through the rind every 6 mm (¼ in) with scissors to prevent the steaks curling up during cooking. Brush the steaks with oil, and grill under the grill for 3 or 4 minutes each side. Brush one side of each steak with honey and grill for another minute. Remove from the grill and let stand for 3 minutes.

Serve with the salsa spooned on top of the ham steaks.

Serves 4

welsh rarebit

see variations page 267

This is sometimes mistakenly called Welsh rabbit. The success of this dish lies in cooking it slowly over a low heat until the cheese has melted.

225g (8oz) good-quality grated Cheddar cheese
25g (1oz) unsalted butter
1 tsp dry mustard powder

3 tbsp beer
salt and freshly ground black pepper to taste
4 slices buttered toast

Preheat the grill. In a medium saucepan, cook the cheese, butter, mustard and beer over a low heat. Season with salt and pepper. Stir occasionally until the mixture is smooth and creamy.

Spoon the cheese mix onto the toast, and put under the grill until golden and bubbling. Serve immediately.

Serves 4

potato hash bake

see variations page 268

This is delicious at a brunch buffet, and you can make it entirely in advance. Just reheat to serve.

25g (1oz) butter, plus extra for greasing
4 large potatoes, peeled and roughly diced
1 tbsp olive oil
225g (8oz) sliced button mushrooms
1 (425g/15oz) tin sweetcorn, drained
4 tomatoes, quartered

1 small onion, finely chopped
6 spring onions, chopped
3 tbsp whipping cream
175g (6oz) grated Cheddar cheese
salt and freshly ground black pepper
3 tbsp freshly chopped parsley, to garnish

Heat the oven to 180°C (350°F/Gas mark 4) and generously grease a large baking dish with butter. In a large saucepan, boil the potatoes for 10-15 minutes until tender. Drain, tip back into the saucepan, and mash. In a medium saucepan, heat 1 tablespoon olive oil, add the mushrooms, and fry over medium heat for a few minutes until lightly browned and cooked through. Add the corn and tomatoes to the pan and stir together for a minute. Set aside.

In a medium frying pan, melt the butter and fry the onion for a few minutes until softened and lightly browned. Tip into the mashed potatoes, with the butter from the pan, and add the chopped spring onions. Mix well. Add cream, and 100g (4oz) of cheese. Season well with salt and freshly ground pepper. Place the mushrooms, corn, and tomatoes in the bottom of the baking dish, and spread the potato-onion mixture on top. Sprinkle the remaining cheese on top and bake in the oven for 20 minutes, or until the cheese has melted and the dish is a lovely golden brown. Serve immediately, sprinkled with a little freshly chopped parsley.

Serves 4

potato cakes with bacon & cheese

see variations page 269

These potato cakes make a delightful side dish, and are delicious served with smoky beans
(page 251) and eggs.

900g (2lb) potatoes
50g (2oz) butter
1 small onion, finely chopped
1 tsp fresh thyme leaves
225g (8oz) green cabbage, finely sliced

2 tbsp double cream
salt and freshly ground black pepper to taste
8 rashers bacon
plain flour, for dusting
4 slices Cheddar cheese

Peel the potatoes, and cut them into even-size chunks. Place them in a large saucepan,
cover with water, and boil for about 20 minutes, until soft. Drain well and return to the
pan. Put back over the heat for a minute, shaking slightly to make sure they are dry. Melt
half the butter in another saucepan, and cook the chopped onion and thyme for about
5 or 6 minutes, until soft. Add the cabbage and a little water. Cover and cook until tender,
then drain and add to the potatoes with the rest of the butter, the cream and plenty of salt
and pepper. Mash the mixture well, divide into four, and shape into large potato cakes. Put
on a greased baking tray and chill in the refrigerator for 1 hour.

Heat a large frying pan, and fry the bacon until crisp. Remove bacon from pan and keep
warm. Dust the potato cakes with flour and fry them in the bacon drippings for about
5 minutes each side, until crisp and golden. Top each cake with a slice of Cheddar cheese
and transfer to a warmed plate. Place the bacon on top of each cake and serve immediately.

Makes 4

potato rosti

see variations page 270

Unlike the sausage & rosti recipe in the last chapter, this rosti uses grated boiled potatoes before being made into a cake shape and baked in the oven. I find oven-baking rosti much easier and quicker than frying it on the stove.

butter, for greasing and for cooking
6 rashers bacon
1.4kg (3lb) red potatoes, peeled

6 tbsp olive oil
1 medium onion, minced and drained of
    moisture

Heat the oven to 190°C (375°F/Gas mark 5) and generously butter a 20-cm (8-in) cake pan with butter. Put a baking tray in the oven to heat.

In a large frying pan, fry the bacon until golden and crisp, remove and drain on paper towels. Break into small pieces.

In a large saucepan, boil the whole potatoes for 5 minutes, drain and drop into iced water. When cold enough to handle, grate the potatoes into a large bowl. Mix in oil gradually, then add the drained onion and bacon pieces. Tip the potato mixture into the cake pan, do not press it down, and dot with butter over the top. Place the pan on the hot baking tray in the oven and bake for 1 hour 20 minutes, until the potatoes are cooked through and crispy on top. Serve immediately, cut into wedges, like slices of cake.

Serves 6-8

hash browns

see variations page 271

These are very similar to rosti, but they're the American version of the Swiss classic. They take a little planning, as you start them the night before.

8 large red potatoes, peeled
2 tsp salt
1 tsp freshly ground black pepper

50g (2oz) butter with a little vegetable
oil added

In a large saucepan, boil the whole potatoes for 15-20 minutes, until just tender. Drain, pat dry and chill in the refrigerator overnight.

The next morning, grate the potatoes into a large bowl, and add the salt and pepper. Heat the butter and vegetable oil in a large frying pan. Add the potatoes and cook for 8-10 minutes, or until golden brown on the bottom. Tip out onto a plate, then slide back into the pan to cook the other side. Cook until golden brown and crispy underneath, about 8-10 minutes. Serve immediately.

Serves 8

chilli cheese breakfast casserole

see variations page 272

There are so many breakfast recipes with potatoes or bread that rice makes a welcome change. Try serving this the next time you have a brunch buffet.

butter, for greasing
225g (8oz) uncooked long-grain white rice
475ml (16fl.oz) water
225g (8oz) cottage cheese
1 (425g/15oz) tin sweetcorn, drained

1 red pepper, finely chopped
1 green pepper, finely chopped
225ml (8fl.oz) soured cream
25g (1oz) finely chopped mild green chillies
225g (8oz) chopped mozzarella

Heat the oven to 180°C (350°F/Gas mark 4) and grease a large baking dish with butter.

In a large saucepan, cook the rice in the water, as directed on the package, usually 10 minutes, until all the water is absorbed. Place the rice in a bowl to cool slightly. Add the cottage cheese, sweetcorn, red and green peppers, sour cream and chillies. Mix well. Put the mixture into the baking dish and sprinkle the cheese over the top. Bake for 30-35 minutes, until thoroughly heated and the cheese has melted. Serve immediately.

Serves 6

wild rice cakes

see variations page 273

These rice cakes are not commonly seen as a breakfast item, but if you are trying to lower your carbohydrate intake, they make a spicy alternative to hash browns. Wear rubber gloves when chopping chillies, because they can irritate your skin.

50g (2oz) uncooked wild rice
475ml (16fl.oz) water
1 tbsp flour
1 tsp baking powder
½ tsp salt
1 mild green chilli, finely chopped

3 tbsp grated onion
1 egg
1 tbsp finely chopped and peeled fresh root ginger
2 tbsp olive oil

In a medium saucepan, boil the rice in the water for about 40 minutes, until tender. Drain and place in a bowl. Sprinkle the flour, baking powder and salt over the rice, and stir until combined.

In a small bowl, whisk together the chilli, onion, egg and ginger, and add to the rice mixture.

In a large frying pan, heat the oil over medium heat. Put 2 tablespoons rice mixture into the pan and shape to form cakes. Cook 4 at a time for 3 minutes on each side, until golden brown. Drain on paper towels. Keep warm while you make the rest. Serve immediately.

Makes 8 cakes

smoky beans with bacon & basil

see variations page 274

Homemade baked beans, served as a delicious accompaniment to eggs or sausages, or as a topping for toast, for a perfect start to the day.

2 tbsp olive oil
1 large onion, finely chopped
1 tsp smoked paprika
2 (425g/15oz) tins cannellini beans, drained
5 large fresh tomatoes, deseeded and chopped

8 rashers bacon
large handful fresh basil leaves
salt and freshly ground black pepper
few shakes of Tabasco sauce

In a medium saucepan, heat the oil and add the onion. Cook over high heat for about 5 minutes until softened and starting to brown. Turn the heat down a little, add the paprika, drained beans and chopped tomatoes to the pan and cook for a few minutes.

In a large frying pan, fry the bacon until crisp and golden, then break into bite-size pieces. Set aside.

Grate the basil and add to the pan with the salt and freshly ground black pepper. Add a few shakes of hot sauce. Continue to cook until the tomatoes have broken down a little and the basil has wilted. Serve immediately, with the bacon sprinkled over the top.

Serves 4

bacon-wrapped portobello mushrooms

see variations page 275

You cook these mushrooms in the oven, but you can also cook them under the grill or on the BBQ. They're great with scrambled eggs and sausages or as part of a breakfast buffet. You could also serve them on toast.

2 tsp vegetable oil, for brushing and greasing
8 large portobello mushrooms
8 rashers bacon

Preheat the oven to 190°C (375°F/Gas mark 5) or preheat the grill. Grease a baking tray with vegetable oil.

Wipe the mushrooms clean, and wrap each one with a bacon rasher. Place on the baking tray and brush lightly with a little vegetable oil. Place in the oven and bake for 10 minutes, until the bacon is crispy. Alternatively, cook under the grill, watching carefully to make sure the bacon does not burn. Serve immediately.

Serves 8

oven-roasted vine tomatoes

see variations page 276

These are so simple to do, and tomatoes take on a completely different flavour when oven-roasted with olive oil. Leaving them on the vine makes them look special.

olive oil for brushing and greasing
16-20 small tomatoes on the vine

3 tsp fresh thyme leaves
salt and freshly ground black pepper to taste

Preheat the oven to 190°C (375°F/Gas mark 5) and grease a baking tray with olive oil.

Keeping the tomatoes on the vine, snip them into groups of 4 or 5. Place on the baking tray, brush the tomatoes carefully with olive oil, and sprinkle the thyme leaves and salt and pepper over them. Bake in the oven for 15-20 minutes, until the tomatoes have softened. Serve immediately.

Serves 4

breakfast wraps

see variations page 277

Wrap up your scrambled eggs in a flour tortilla to take with you to eat on the way to work or school. Tortillas come in different sizes, so you can make your sandwich any size you want.

2 tsp vegetable oil
3 eggs
salt and freshly ground black pepper
125g (4oz) chopped ham

2 tbsp finely chopped green pepper
3 tbsp grated Cheddar cheese
2 flour tortillas

In a large frying pan, heat a little vegetable oil. In a medium bowl, whisk the eggs, season with salt and pepper to taste, and stir in the ham and green pepper. Pour into the frying pan and stir with a wooden spoon to scramble the eggs. Cook until almost set, add the cheese, and cook for another minute or until the cheese is melted.

Heat the tortillas by steaming them in the microwave in moist paper towels (or use a tortilla steamer) for 30 seconds. Spoon the filling into the middle of each tortilla. Roll up and serve immediately.

Serves 2

breakfast sausage burger with bacon & cheese

see variations page 278

Very similar to fast food, but much better homemade.

450g (1lb) pork sausage
1 tbsp fresh thyme leaves
2 tsp freshly ground black pepper
2 tbsp vegetable oil

8 rashers bacon
4 slices cheese
4 hamburger buns, split

Preheat the grill and preheat the oven to 170°C (325°F/Gas mark 3). Put 4 serving plates in the oven to warm. In a large bowl, mix the sausage with the thyme leaves and black pepper. Form into 4 patties. In a large frying pan, heat the oil, and fry the patties for a few minutes until golden brown and cooked through. Drain on paper towels.

Put the bacon in the frying pan and fry for a few minutes until crisp and cooked through. Remove and drain on paper towels. Place the hamburger halves on a baking tray and grill until golden brown.

Assemble the burgers. Put the bottom half of the buns on warm serving plates. Put a sausage patty on each bun and top with a slice of cheese and 2 rashers of bacon placed across the cheese. Put the top half of the buns on top and put the plates back in the oven for 3 minutes to heat through and to slightly melt the cheese. Serve immediately.

Serves 4

bacon sandwich with apple & blue cheese

see variations page 279

Is there anything more evocative of lazy weekend mornings than the scent of frying bacon? Here is a bacon sandwich with a twist—the flavours go really well together, and create a satisfying sandwich that will fill you up all morning.

2 tsp vegetable oil
10 rashers bacon (or 6 rashers back bacon)
1 apple, peeled, cored, and sliced

4 thick slices white bread
butter, for spreading
25g (1oz) Stilton or other blue cheese

In a large frying pan, melt the oil and fry the bacon over medium heat for about 3-4 minutes each side, until crisp and golden. Add the apple slices to the pan and sauté over a medium heat for 3 minutes, or until golden and tender. Remove from heat.

Spread the bread with butter, and divide the bacon and apple between two slices. Crumble the blue cheese over the top, and place the other 2 slices of bread on top. Serve immediately.

Serves 2

mini breakfast calzones

see variations page 280

Mini calzones are delicious, filling, and easily portable if needed.

for the dough
1 tsp sugar
300ml (10fl.oz) lukewarm water
1 envelope active dried yeast
450g (1lb) white bread flour
1 level tsp salt
1 tbsp olive oil

for the filling
2 tsp vegetable oil
450g (1lb) pork sausage, crumbled
1 small onion, chopped
2 tsp dried basil
2 tsp dried oregano
50g (2oz) tomato pizza sauce

Prepare the yeast liquid by dissolving the sugar in the warm water. Sprinkle the yeast on top and leave until frothy, about 10 minutes. Sift the flour and salt into a large bowl, make a well in the centre, and add the yeast liquid and olive oil together. Work to a firm dough, turn onto a lightly floured surface, and knead thoroughly with your hands and knuckles until you have a soft, smooth, and elastic dough. Alternatively, knead the dough in a freestanding tabletop mixer for 5 minutes. Put the dough into a greased bowl, turning to coat it all over, and cover with clingfilm. Let rise in a warm place until doubled in size.

While the dough is rising, make the filling. In a large frying pan, heat a little oil, add the crumbled sausage, and cook until it is no longer pink. Add the chopped onion and fry for a few minutes until the mixture is cooked and browned. Add the basil, oregano, and pizza sauce. Stir to mix well and set aside to cool completely.

Turn the dough onto a lightly floured surface and knock back slightly. Divide into 18 pieces, shaping into balls. Roll out the balls to a 15-cm (6-in) circle and place 1 tablespoon filling in the middle. Slightly wet the edges and gather the edges together at the top to enclose the filling. Turn the rolls upside down and roll out slightly, pressing them down gently without forcing the filling out. Place on floured baking trays, with the seam underneath, dust with flour, cover loosely, and let rise until doubled in size. Heat the oven to 220°C (425°F/Gas mark 7). Remove the covering and bake the rolls for 15-20 minutes. Remove from the oven and cool slightly on a wire rack.

Makes 18

breakfast burritos

see variations page 281

Ready for breakfast Tex-Mex style?

2 tsp vegetable oil
175g (6oz) pork sausage, chopped
2 tbsp finely chopped onion
1 tbsp finely chopped mild or hot green chilli
4 eggs, beaten

salt and freshly ground black pepper
4 large (25cm/10in) tortillas
4 slices mild processed cheese
salsa and guacamole, to serve

Heat oil in a frying pan over medium heat, then crumble the sausage into the pan. Add the onion. Cook for 5 minutes until the sausage is browned and the onion is softened and lightly coloured. Add the chopped chilli, stir for another minute, and then add the beaten eggs. Scramble using a wooden spoon until the eggs begin to set. Season with salt and pepper and remove from heat.

Heat the tortillas either by steaming in the microwave in moist paper towels, or in a tortilla steamer, for 30 seconds. Break each slice of cheese in half and place end to end in the middle of each tortilla. Spoon a quarter of the egg filling on top of the cheese on each of the tortillas. Fold one side of each tortilla over the filling, then fold up about 5cm (2in) of one end. Fold over the other side of the tortilla to complete the burritos, leaving one end open. Serve immediately, with a little salsa and guacamole on the side.

Serves 4

pork sausages

see base recipe page 233

lincolnshire sausages
Prepare the basic recipe, adding 1 tablespoon freshly chopped parsley,
1 tablespoon freshly chopped sage, and 1 tablespoon fresh thyme leaves to
the mixture.

cumberland sausages
Prepare the basic recipe, adding 1 tablespoon freshly ground black pepper
to the mixture, and when shaping the sausage, make it into a long
circular spiral.

pork & leek sausages
Prepare the basic recipe, adding 1 cooked, well-drained, and finely chopped leek
to the mixture.

spicy peri-peri sausages
Prepare the basic recipe, adding ½ teaspoon peri-peri sauce to the mixture.
Adjust the amount to your own personal taste.

pork & apple sausages
Prepare the basic recipe, adding 2 peeled, cored, and chopped Granny Smith
apples to the meat mixture.

gammon with pineapple salsa

see base recipe page 234

gammon with pineapple & red pepper salsa
Prepare the basic recipe, adding 1 teaspoon crushed red pepper flakes to the salsa.

orange-glazed gammon with pineapple salsa
Prepare the basic recipe, replacing the honey with orange marmalade.

gammon with pineapple & pear salsa
Prepare the basic recipe, adding 1 pear, peeled, cored and chopped, to the salsa.

mustard-glazed gammon & poached eggs
Prepare the basic recipe, replacing the honey with honey mustard. Instead of serving with salsa, serve with poached eggs (page 155).

juice-marinated gammon with pineapple salsa
Prepare the basic recipe, but marinate the gammon in a little apple juice for an hour before cooking.

welsh rarebit

see base recipe page 237

welsh rarebit with worcestershire sauce
Prepare the basic recipe, adding 2 teaspoons Worcestershire sauce to
the cheese.

welsh rarebit with poached eggs
Prepare the basic recipe, and add a poached egg (page 155) on top of the
rarebit, just before serving.

welsh rarebit with herbs
Prepare the basic recipe, adding 1 tablespoon freshly chopped mixed herbs to
the cheese.

potato hash bake

see base recipe page 238

potato hash bake with bacon
Prepare the basic recipe, adding 4 rashers chopped bacon to the pan with the mushrooms, and sauté until crisp.

potato hash bake with swiss cheese
Prepare the basic recipe, replacing the Cheddar cheese with Gruyère cheese.

potato hash bake with pancetta
Prepare the basic recipe, adding 75g (3oz) chopped pancetta to the pan with the mushrooms.

potato hash bake with asparagus
Prepare the basic recipe, adding a few spears of steamed asparagus to the vegetables in the bottom of the baking dish.

potato hash bake with salmon
Prepare the basic recipe, adding 1 lightly poached salmon fillet to the pan with the vegetables.

variations

potato cakes with bacon & cheese

see base recipe page 240

potato cakes with cod & parsley
Prepare the basic recipe, omitting the cabbage and thyme, and replacing them with 275g (10oz) cooked, boneless, flaked cod and freshly chopped parsley. Top with the cheese and bacon, if desired.

salmon potato cakes
Prepare the basic recipe, omitting the cabbage and thyme, and substituting with 275g (10oz) of boneless, flaked salmon fillet, and freshly chopped parsley. Top with the cheese and bacon, if desired.

potato cakes with bacon & swiss cheese
Prepare the basic recipe, replacing the Cheddar cheese with sliced Swiss cheese.

spicy potato cakes
Prepare the basic recipe, adding 2 teaspoons crushed red chilli pepper flakes to the potato mixture.

potato cakes with crab
Prepare the basic recipe, replacing the cabbage with 275g (10oz) cooked, canned or fresh, boneless, flaked crabmeat. Top with the cheese and bacon, if desired.

variations

potato rosti

see base recipe page 243

italian potato rosti
Prepare the basic recipe, adding 3 teaspoons dried Italian herbs to the frying pan with the onion.

mexican potato rosti
Prepare the basic recipe, adding 1 tablespoon crushed dried red pepper flakes to the frying pan with the onion.

potato rosti with pancetta
Prepare the basic recipe, adding 50g (2oz) chopped pancetta to the frying pan with the onion.

french potato rosti
Prepare the basic recipe, adding 1 crushed clove of garlic to the frying pan with the onion.

potato & parsnip rosti
Prepare the basic recipe, replacing a third of the potato with parsnips.

variations

hash browns

see base recipe page 244

spicy hash browns
Prepare the basic recipe, adding 1 teaspoon Cajun seasoning and
1/4 teaspoon cayenne pepper to the potatoes with the salt and pepper.

hash browns with cheese
Prepare the basic recipe. Ten minutes before the end of cooking, sprinkle
50g (2oz) grated Cheddar cheese over the potatoes.

hash browns with bacon
Prepare the basic recipe, adding 5 rashers of bacon, cooked until crisp, and
crumbled, to the potatoes with the salt and pepper.

hash browns with chilli
Prepare the basic recipe, adding 2 teaspoons dried crushed red chilli flakes
to the potatoes with the salt and pepper.

red flannel hash
Prepare the basic recipe, adding 1 boiled and chopped beetroot to the
potatoes with the salt and pepper.

variations

chilli cheese breakfast casserole

see base recipe page 247

chilli cheese & bacon breakfast casserole
Prepare the basic recipe, adding 4 rashers cooked and crispy bacon.

chilli cheese & tomato breakfast casserole
Prepare the basic recipe, adding 2 seeded and chopped tomatoes.

chilli swiss cheese breakfast casserole
Prepare the basic recipe, replacing the Monterey Jack cheese with
Gruyère cheese.

chilli cheese & parma breakfast casserole
Prepare the basic recipe, adding 75g (3oz) chopped Parma ham.

chilli cheese & chorizo breakfast casserole
Prepare the basic recipe, replacing the cheese with spicy cheese.
Add a few jalapeños and 50g (2oz) chopped chorizo.

variations

wild rice cakes

see base recipe page 248

smoky wild rice & bulgur wheat cakes with smoked salmon
Prepare the basic recipe, replacing half the wild rice with 50g (2oz) cooked
bulgur wheat. Add 2 teaspoons smoked paprika to the rice mixture. Top
with a thin slice of smoked salmon and serve accompanied by a slice of
fresh lemon.

wild rice cakes with tomato
Prepare the basic recipe, adding 1 seeded and chopped tomato to the
rice mixture.

rice cakes with wild mushrooms
Prepare the basic recipe, replacing half the wild rice with 75g (3oz) cooked
brown rice. Add 50g (2oz) very finely chopped wild mushrooms to the
rice mixture.

wild rice cakes with cheese & chives
Prepare the basic recipe, adding 50g (2oz) grated Cheddar cheese and
2 tablespoons freshly chopped chives to the rice mixture.

wild rice cakes with poached egg & herbs
Prepare the basic recipe, and add 2 tablespoons crushed mixed herbs to the
rice mixture. Serve topped with poached eggs (page 155).

variations

smoky beans with bacon & basil

see base recipe page 251

quick smoky beans with apple
Instead of the basic recipe, in a large baking dish, mix together
2 (450-g/16-oz) cans baked beans, 1 peeled and chopped Granny Smith
apple, 1 tablespoon Dijon mustard, 4 tablespoons ketchup, 1 tablespoon
Worcestershire sauce, and 50g (2oz) brown sugar. Heat until just simmering,
then bake at 180°C (350°F/Gas mark 4) for 25 minutes until the apple is
tender. Serve immediately, with crisp, crumbled bacon sprinkled on top.

smoky beans with celery, chorizo & basil
Prepare the basic recipe, replacing the bacon with 100g (4oz) chopped
chorizo. Add 1 stick chopped celery with the chopped tomatoes.

smoky black beans with bacon, peppers & basil
Prepare the basic recipe, replacing the cannellini beans with canned black
beans. Add 1 chopped green pepper to the frying pan and cook with the
onion until tender.

smoky beans with parma ham & coriander
Prepare the basic recipe, replacing the bacon with Parma ham and the basil
with coriander.

variations

bacon-wrapped portobello mushrooms

see base recipe page 252

herbed bacon-wrapped portobellos
Prepare the basic recipe, and sprinkle 2 tablespoons chopped mixed fresh herbs over the mushrooms before cooking.

cajun-spiced bacon-wrapped portobellos
Prepare the basic recipe, and sprinkle 1 tablespoon Cajun seasoning over the mushrooms before cooking.

sweet & spicy bacon-wrapped portobellos
Prepare the basic recipe, sprinkling the mushrooms before cooking with a mixture of 1 tablespoon brown sugar and 1 teaspoon mild chilli powder.

bacon-wrapped portobellos with cheese
Prepare the basic recipe, and sprinkle on a little finely grated Parmesan cheese before cooking.

pancetta-wrapped portobellos
Prepare the basic recipe, replacing the bacon with pancetta.

oven-roasted vine tomatoes

see base recipe page 254

oven-roasted vine tomatoes with garlic
Prepare the basic recipe, adding 1 crushed garlic clove to the thyme before sprinkling it over the tomatoes.

oven-roasted vine tomatoes with walnuts
Prepare the basic recipe, brushing the tomatoes with walnut oil instead of olive oil and adding 2 tablespoons finely chopped walnuts to the thyme before sprinkling it over the tomatoes.

oven-roasted vine tomatoes with oregano & basil
Prepare the basic recipe, replacing the fresh thyme leaves with freshly chopped oregano and basil.

oven-roasted vine tomatoes with pesto
Prepare the basic recipe, omitting the fresh thyme leaves. Instead of brushing tomatoes with olive oil, brush them with 4 teaspoons pesto.

oven-roasted vine tomatoes with parmesan cheese
Prepare the basic recipe, adding a sprinkling of Parmesan cheese on the tomatoes 10 minutes before the end of cooking time.

breakfast wraps

see base recipe page 257

breakfast wraps with tomato
Prepare the basic recipe, adding 3 tomatoes, seeded and chopped, to
the filling.

breakfast wraps with feta cheese
Prepare the basic recipe, adding 75g (3oz) feta cheese to the filling.

breakfast wraps with feta, olives & mint
Prepare the basic recipe, omitting the Cheddar cheese and substituting
75g (3oz) feta cheese, 2 tablespoons pitted and chopped black olives, and
1 tablespoons freshly chopped mint to the filling.

breakfast wraps with bacon
Prepare the basic recipe, adding 4 rashers of bacon, cooked until crispy and
broken into small pieces, to the filling.

breakfast wraps with chillies
Prepare the basic recipe, adding 2 tablespoons chopped, canned jalapeño
peppers to the filling.

variations

breakfast sausage burger with bacon & cheese

see base recipe page 258

spicy sausage burger with bacon & cheese
Prepare the basic recipe, adding 1 teaspoon ground cumin to the sausage mixture.

hot sausage burger with bacon & cheese
Prepare the basic recipe, adding half a chopped hot green chilli to the sausage during mixing.

italian sausage burger with bacon & cheese
Prepare the basic recipe, replacing the thyme leaves in the sausage mixture with 2 teaspoons dried oregano and 2 teaspoons dried basil.

egg sausage burger on sourdough
Prepare the basic recipe, replacing the hamburger buns with 8 slices of sourdough bread. Add a poached or fried egg on top of the sausage on each burger.

breakfast sausage & onion burger with bacon & cheese
Prepare the basic recipe, adding 4 spring onions, finely chopped, to the sausage mixture.

bacon sandwich with apple & blue cheese

see base recipe page 261

bacon sandwich with fried egg & brown sauce
Make the variation above, adding a fried egg to each sandwich. Add
1–2 teaspoons brown sauce to each sandwich.

bacon sandwich with apple & cheddar
Prepare the basic recipe, replacing the blue cheese with grated
Cheddar cheese.

bacon sandwich with pear & blue cheese
Prepare the basic recipe, replacing the apple with a pear.

bacon sandwich with apple & dill pickle
Prepare the basic recipe, replacing the blue cheese with a few slices of
dill pickle.

bacon sandwich with tomato & tomato chutney
Prepare the basic recipe, omitting the apple and blue cheese and
substituting a few slices of tomato and 2–3 teaspoons tomato chutney
on each sandwich.

variations

mini breakfast calzones

see base recipe page 262

quick mini breakfast calzones
Prepare the basic recipe, but instead of making the dough, use purchased 450g (1lb) refrigerated pizza dough.

mini breakfast calzones with chorizo
Prepare the basic recipe, replacing the sausage with finely chopped chorizo.

mini breakfast calzones with eggs
Prepare the basic recipe, adding 2 chopped hard-boiled eggs to the filling.

mini breakfast calzones with sausage & eggs
Prepare the basic recipe, but use purchased pizza dough rolled into 15-cm (6-in) circles. Omit onion, herbs, and pizza sauce. Cook sausage and sprinkle onto pizza circle. Top with well-seasoned, lightly scrambled eggs and slices of your favourite cheese. Fold over half the dough, seal edges, and bake at 220°C (425°F/Gas mark 7) for about 15–20 minutes.

mini breakfast calzones with sun-dried tomatoes
Prepare the basic recipe, adding 50g (2oz) chopped sun-dried tomatoes to the filling.

breakfast burritos

see base recipe page 264

breakfast burritos with refried beans
Prepare the basic recipe, omitting the filling. Make a filling from 50g (2oz) refried beans, crumbled crisp bacon, a little arugula, and 50g (2oz) grated spicy cheese. Spoon salsa on top of the filling before rolling.

egg-wrapped breakfast burritos
Prepare the basic recipe, omitting the flour tortillas. Make the wraps out of omelets. For each wrap, use 1 egg, swirled around in the frying pan to make it as thin as possible.

egg-wrapped vegetarian breakfast burrito
Use the egg wrap from the variation above. Use the refried bean filling, without the bacon, from the refried bean variation.

breakfast burritos with ham & swiss
Prepare the basic recipe, omitting the sausage and its cooking step and substituting 75g (3oz) chopped ham. Replace the processed cheese with Swiss cheese.

index